To

_____

From

_____

Date

_____

Come Sit a Spell

COME SIT A SPELL

An invitation to reflect on faith, food, and family

MARILYN JANSEN

Tyndale House Publishers
Carol Stream, Illinois

Visit Tyndale online at tyndale.com.

Visit the author's website at marilynjansen.com.

Tyndale, Tyndale's quill logo, *Living Expressions*, and the Living Expressions logo are registered trademarks of Tyndale House Ministries.

Come Sit a Spell: An Invitation to Reflect on Faith, Food, and Family

Designed by Jacqueline L. Nuñez

Published in association with the literary agency of Books & Such Literary Management

For information about special discounts for bulk purchases, please contact Tyndale House Publishers at csresponse@tyndale.com, or call 1-855-277-9400.

ISBN 978-1-4964-5367-9

Printed in China

28	27	26	25	24	23	22
7	6	5	4	3	2	1

CONTENTS

PART 2: COME SIT A SPELL AT MOM'S

PART 3: COME SIT A SPELL WITH ME

INTRODUCTION
When We All Get Together

The kitchen table was loaded with
enough food to bury the family.
HARPER LEE, *To Kill a Mockingbird*

I grew up a southern Missouri hillbilly. From the time I was eight until I was eighteen, I lived down a long gravel road that crossed through two creeks, snug up against some of the tallest hills in Missouri, deep in the Mark Twain National Forest. My mom, stepdad, two brothers, sister, and I had a home in the same holler as Grandma and Grandpa Dunn's hundred-year-old farmhouse.

We raised vegetables in huge family gardens, slaughtered chickens and pigs every fall, and put up hundreds of jars of vittles for the year to come. We rarely wore shoes (except Uncle Bill, who according to Mom was too stuck-up to go barefoot), could spit watermelon seeds might near a mile, and boiled up some of the best maple syrup in the county. Lightning bugs lit up summer nights, and woodstoves warmed winter fingers blue with cold from outdoor chores.

We didn't have much money, but we waded into each new day with faith, joy, and expectation, like it was the last day of summer and the creek might dry up tomorrow. There was always something to discover and someone with a story or two. And oh, how I love stories. I never wanted to miss a thing. I would squeeze between two aunts or sit beside Grandma's

1

chair, catching every word they dropped during those big Sunday dinners after church.

When people came to Grandma's house—just a hop, a skip, and three jumps from ours—I would run to meet them at her door. On weekends and holidays, Grandma's kitchen was beautiful chaos. The number of aunts, uncles, cousins, and kids in her kitchen at mealtimes rivaled the number of Carnival glass dishes displayed in her curved-front china cabinet. In her kitchen we received "bless your heart" squeezes, wiped away smooches, and tried to avoid the oh-too-often snap on the behind from a wicked dish towel.

The food was abundant and finger-licking good. We enjoyed wafer cookies washed down with spring water gulped from a dipper that hung on a nail just above the sink, where you could grab it without looking. Every Sunday, we would eat in waves, scooching over to make room for more on the bench until we were hanging on with one cheek. I don't remember ever having fewer than four different kinds of food on the table during a meal, often as many as twelve or more. It wasn't fancy food. It was humble and simple and comforted us plumb down to our toes. With so many bowls on the table, I expected it to buckle under the weight. I remember looking at its underside to see if it was bowed in the middle or propped up on cinder blocks.

Grandma, in her housedress and stockings, would be standing near the sink looking around to make sure everyone had something to eat. With her hand supporting her back and a sparkle in her eye, she ruled the roost. I felt part of something special there, like I was known and really, truly loved. My heart was fuller than my belly.

Mom's kitchen was just as welcoming but in a different way. We hosted the city cousins and whoever else wanted to *come sit a spell*. Mom and Aunt Jean would make homemade barbecue sauce, simmering it all day in a tall pan on a grill that alternately charred ribs, pork steaks, and chicken. There were tubs of homemade potato salad; fresh greens wilted with bacon grease; and platters of sliced, fresh-from-the-garden cucumbers and tomatoes. Games of horseshoes would strike up outside and cards at the kitchen table, and when someone showed up with an amplifier, it was a party. It wasn't unusual to have a preacher and some drunk uncle or cousin in the same crowd. Everyone was welcome. We drank gallons of sweet tea, laughed till our sides split, and were happier than foxes in a henhouse.

Because I grew up in that atmosphere of joy and love, I wanted to carry on the traditions. I don't have the clamor nor the china cabinet, but I seem to have perfected the chaos. In my kitchen someone is usually sticking a finger or spoon in whatever is on the stove or opening the oven a smidge to peep inside. Dancing, heart-to-heart talks, unbridled laughter, and put-that-down-and-tell-me-the-whole-story moments often happen when people come sit a spell in my kitchen.

It's not surprising that God wants the same thing. He asks us to come to His table and discover the love, hope, and joy that we were born to find. He knows the value of a good story, the warmth of simply being with family, and the bonds that grow when we sit together over a cup of coffee or a game of Scrabble.

When you boil it down, the kitchen isn't the important

thing, nor is the food (although if you don't like food, I'm not sure we could be friends). Relationships are what bring us to the gathering places—the beautiful soul-knowing that comes from sitting eyeball-to-eyeball and experiencing each other. Knowing and being known.

God is inviting you in (Revelation 3:20). Won't you come sit a spell?

Part 1

COME SIT A SPELL AT GRANDMA'S

It was a good moment, the kind you would like to press between the pages of a book, or hide in your sock drawer, so you could touch it again.

RICK BRAGG,
All Over but the Shoutin'

TIME TO PLUCK THE CHICKENS

If anyone is not willing to work, let him not eat.
2 THESSALONIANS 3:10, ESV

One of the happy places I retreat to in my mind when I'm feeling sad or overwhelmed with work is my Grandma Dunn's kitchen. I practically lived in that kitchen. She almost always had something cooking—a pot of beans, a pan of corn-bread, a pineapple upside-down cake, a kettle of chicken and dumplins. And there were always side dishes in some level of preparation, lots and lots of sides: fresh tomato slices, crocks of apple butter, crisp green beans, fried potatoes, coleslaw . . .

She and Grandpa—Mom's parents—lived on a farm that basically rendered them self-sufficient. All Grandma needed was some flour and sugar, an occasional visit from the Watkins man, and a delivery of baby chicks every spring. Those cute babies would come in a cardboard box with holes cut into the top and sides, then go into a small pen on Grandma's porch. They had a light for warmth, a little divided tin bowl for chicken feed, and an upside-down jar with a dispenser lid for water. On cold spring mornings I would find them sleeping away, all huddled together under the light, nary a peep from the whole crew. But the clamor that came when they awoke and fought for a place at the front of the food line was a horse of a differ-ent color . . . or sound.

When old enough, the chicks would be moved into the chicken coop, where they would scratch the ground, chase insects, and grow into the birds that would lay eggs and eventually be put up for winter food. I threw handfuls of tiny chicken-pellet food over the fence into their pen and collected their eggs. In the fall, we would gather at Grandma's to butcher the chickens and clean them in her kitchen.

My mom was a champion chicken killer. The idea was to kill them quickly and efficiently. We loved our animals, but we were farmers and poor people who relied on the meat they provided. When it was time, Mom would grab a chicken in each hand and, with one smooth motion, wring both their necks. She was merciful. I tried to do the same, but I was more like a chicken torturer, so I was given other jobs—like cleaning them. I hated the plucking, but I did it without too much whining because I knew we would take one of those big fat hens and boil it up with dumplins.

After the chickens were plucked, we took a match to the remaining little baby-hair feathers to singe them off before washing and freezing the hens. That is not a smell you will ever forget, let me tell ya.

If we wanted dumplins, we had to clean chickens. If I had my druthers, I would have napped with the cat during that part. But my family embraced this idea from the Bible: "If anyone is not willing to work, let him not eat" (2 Thessalonians 3:10, ESV). Though I didn't have a choice, knowing that soon the spewy sound of Grandma's pressure cooker would be ticking away on the stove made it worth it.

The fun part of making chicken and dumplins was the

dumplins. Once the chicken was cooked and the lid came off the pressure cooker, Grandma would start making the pillowy delights. I remember her rolling them out on her counter and seeing wisps of flour dust wafting through the sunshine that streamed in from the window. I pestered Grandma all the time until she let me help her make them. We rolled them out and cut them, then dropped them into the bubbling broth one by one until I thought the pot would overflow.

Grandma's dumplins were incredible. I make her recipe from time to time, and it brings all the memories back. I can never quite capture the taste or feeling that came from her kitchen. I don't have the farm-fresh chickens or the pressure cooker . . . or her.

Plucking chickens did teach me an important lesson: Sometimes you have to work through stinky stuff before you get to enjoy your favorite things. Do the stinky work.

Father, thank You for the work You have given me to do. Lord, help me to do that work—be it easy or stinky—with gratitude and humility.

GRANDMA DUNN'S CHICKEN AND DUMPLINS

This is the recipe I helped Grandma make many times, especially in the fall when we butchered the chickens. I loved dropping the dumplins into the broth and going back to the floury countertop for more.

Ingredients

Broth
1 whole chicken, cut into eight pieces (or 8 pieces dark meat)
12 cups water
1 teaspoon sage
1 teaspoon rosemary
1 teaspoon salt
3 carrots, peeled and cut into 1-inch chunks
1 small onion, sliced
2 tablespoons bouillon

Dumplins
1 cup broth from pot, cooled
2 eggs
4 cups of self-rising flour (extra for rolling surface)

Instructions

1. Put all the broth ingredients except bouillon into a large pot and bring to a boil. Reduce heat and skim foam off the top. Cover and simmer for an hour.
2. Using a colander, strain broth. Remove chicken to cool.
3. Set aside 1 cup of broth to cool for dumplins. Return remaining broth to pot. Add water if necessary to make 10 cups of broth.
4. Pull chicken from bones and shred or chop into bite-sized pieces. Set aside. Add bouillon to the broth. Turn heat to a low simmer.
5. Make dumplins. When the set-aside broth is cool, whisk in eggs and stir in flour. It will be sticky but should hold together.
6. Turn dough out onto a floured surface. Knead a few times, adding in flour to make a soft disk.
7. Roll dough out to make a 24-by-24-inch square. Use plenty of flour to keep the dough from sticking. Cut into 2-inch strips. Then cut strips every 1 inch to make 2-by-1-inch rectangles.
8. With your pastry scraper or spatula, drop dumplins into the broth a few at a time, stirring gently after each addition.
9. Stir half of the shredded chicken meat back into the pot (save the rest for another recipe). Simmer for at least 10 minutes. Serves 8.

ENGLISH JOKER

*This is my prayer: that your love may abound more and more
in knowledge and depth of insight, so that you may be able
to discern what is best and may be pure
and blameless for the day of Christ.*
PHILIPPIANS 1:9-10, NIV

According to the service where I have registered my DNA, I am 100 percent English. That makes sense when you realize the area where I grew up boasts a dialect similar to Elizabethan English. What I would identify as a hillbilly accent, according to some language experts, could be heard at the Globe Theatre in Shakespeare's day. I couldn't imagine Grandma and Grandpa spoutin' lines from *King Lear*. But that would have been something! They apparently had the accent for it.

Being rather isolated, my ancestors and their neighbors kept the phrases, accents, and practices of their heritage longer than folks in other places. They were more Old World than the melting pots of urban areas and passed on some Old English customs. One of those, a shivaree, is a tradition rumored to have spread from England to parts of America and Canada. Basically, it is a noisy celebration sprung on newlyweds without warning. Aunts, uncles, cousins, friends, and others swept up in the chaos surprise the unsuspecting couple the first night they spend in their home.

When I was five or six, I partook in my first shivaree. We sneaked into the bride and groom's yard just before dark with pots and pans and every kind of noisemaker. Then on someone's whispered count, we went to whoopin' and hollerin' and bangin' those pots together like we done escaped from the loony bin. We liked to scared the daylights out of those newlyweds. Then in high shivaree fashion, we sang, laughed, and rooted out some food and drink from the beaming couple. It was all in good fun.

I attended another shivaree the summer I was ten years old. The bride was my aunt. I don't rightly remember whether it was my grandpa, one of the uncles, or one of my older cousins, but some guilty party outfitted me with a smoke bomb. I sure wouldn't have had the ability or the funds to procure a smoke bomb on my own. It was early July, so the bomb itself probably came from one of the city cousins who had brought fireworks down for the Fourth of July celebrations. Anyhow, someone put me up to lighting that sucker at the shivaree.

After the whoopin' and singin', I found my way to the screened-in porch, lit that smoke bomb with matches I had found by the woodstove, and rolled it under the rocking chair. Smoke and hillbillies came pouring out of that house faster than you can say scat. It was a sight to behold. But the look on the older folks' faces let me know pretty quick that I did not want to claim responsibility for this birdbrained idea. Luckily for me, no one was really upset once they realized the house wasn't actually on fire. But I felt the heaviness of guilt from being talked into the prank, mostly because it didn't take much convincing.

Discernment is something most of us have to grow into. The more brothers (or ornery grandpas or uncles or cousins) you have, the faster you grow. We're all gullible at first. The blame is with the ones who put us up to no good. They know the truth but withhold it. The blame becomes ours when we refuse to see the truth.

The Bible advises, "Use your head—and heart!—to discern what is right, to test what is authentically right" (John 7:24, MSG). It is easy to lay blame on others. But at some point, we need to take responsibility for whom we listen to and follow.

The smoke bomb wasn't my idea. A few wily knuckleheads tricked me into it. Ultimately, though, it was my choice. As a child, I depended on my kinfolk having good sense. That may have been a slight miscalculation. As an adult, I know to do the research, test the sources, and accept the responsibility of my choices.

I haven't participated in a shivaree since I've become an adult. My Old English roots are now evidenced through Earl Grey tea and Regency romances. But every once in a while, an "I'll swan!" will slip out in a slightly English accent . . .

Thank You, Lord, for the wisdom to make good decisions. Help me to use my background, experiences, Your Word, and prayer to discern Your truth. If others point me in the wrong direction, help me have the sense and strength to follow You instead.

ENGLISH WALNUT SHORTBREAD

This is my favorite cookie recipe. I make it with whatever nuts are available. Pistachios are exceptionally good in this recipe, but more expensive English walnuts celebrate my heritage.

Ingredients

1½ cups walnuts
2 cups all-purpose flour
¾ teaspoon salt
½ teaspoon cardamom
1 cup unsalted butter, softened
3 ounces cream cheese, softened
⅔ cup sugar
1 tablespoon vanilla extract
1 teaspoon orange zest

Instructions

1. Preheat oven to 350 degrees.
2. Coarsely chop ¾ cup of the nuts and bake for approximately 5 minutes until the nuts are fragrant. Remove nuts from oven and transfer to a bowl to cool. Turn off oven.
3. In a separate bowl, whisk the flour, salt, and cardamom together. Set aside.
4. Using a hand mixer, combine butter and cream cheese in a medium bowl until light and fluffy, approximately 2 minutes on medium speed.
5. Add the sugar, vanilla, and orange zest, and beat for an additional minute. Reduce speed to low and slowly add in flour mixture until just combined. Using a spoon, fold in the cooled toasted nuts.
6. Form cookie dough into an 8-inch log, rolling into plastic wrap. Seal and refrigerate for 4 hours or overnight.
7. Remove dough from refrigerator. Preheat oven to 350 degrees. Finely chop the remaining ¾ cup nuts.
8. Unwrap dough and roll the log in the chopped nuts, coating entirely. Slice cookies into quarter-inch rounds. Place sliced cookies on a parchment-covered baking sheet 1 inch apart.
9. Bake cookies for 18–20 minutes, until the edges are slightly golden brown. Remove baking sheet from oven and let cookies rest for a minute or two. Transfer cookies to a rack and cool completely. Makes about 2½ dozen.

Walnuts and pears you
plant for your heirs.

ENGLISH PROVERB

WHITTLIN' AWAY

These trials will show that your faith is genuine.
It is being tested as fire tests and purifies gold—
though your faith is far more precious than mere gold.

1 PETER 1:7

Grandpa Dunn had a shady spot behind the washhouse, facing the pond, where he would sit and whittle away the afternoon. On summer mornings while Grandma was feeding laundry through the wringer washer in the washhouse, the area was bathed in sunlight, which was perfect for hanging the clothes out to dry.

But in the late afternoons, the area was a cool, shady haven. Grandpa would search the woodpile for a piece that struck his fancy before heading to the shade. He would sit in a discarded kitchen chair that he leaned up against the washhouse wall, pull out his pocketknife, and start shucking the outer bark. The thought of sitting still for that long bored me to tears. But I did try to sit a spell and watch the process a few times.

"Whatcha making, Grandpa?"

"Whatever the wood tells me."

"The wood talks?"

"I reckon it does. I kinda whittle away the extra stuff until the shape inside decides what it wants to be."

It must have taken a long time for that wood to make up its mind, because every time I checked in, it was still a pointy stick. The idea that a work of art was inside a cedar sapling, just waiting to come out, was too complex a concept for me to grasp at the time.

Now I understand art a little better. Layer by layer, an image appears, whether it is through brushstrokes, chisel marks, pencil scratchings, or piping bags. Raw materials give way to the artist's vision, or a close proximity thereof. But everything starts formless.

Grandpa wasn't what you would call a consummate whittler, but it wasn't for lack of trying. Grandma said that he was just *piddlin' around*. She would shoo him from her kitchen whenever he riled her up. He had a habit of putting his fingers in her pies or cuttin' into supper before the lunch dishes were done. But I like to think of him as an artist who was trying valiantly to find the art within the wood.

Michelangelo said, "The sculpture is already complete within the marble block, before I start my work. It is already there; I just have to chisel away the superfluous material." Sounds like what Grandpa was doing—a hillbilly Michelangelo.

Our family has always been creative. We've been crafters, quilters, painters, writers, and bakers for generations. We know what it is to have a vision and see that vision come to life.

But I identify more with the sapling than the artist most of the time. When I sat there with Grandpa all those years ago, I was a formless block. The real me was yet to be determined. God had a vision for how I was to emerge, and He used daily life, experience, time, and relationships to shape who I ultimately became.

The Bible uses a variety of illustrations to describe how God molds us. He purifies us like fire purifies precious metals (1 Peter 1:7). He prunes us as a gardener prunes vines that need to be carefully tended (John 15:2). In order to bring out the image that has been hidden inside, He washes away impurities, removes excess, reshapes, builds, and polishes us until we shine.

Sometimes that shaping hurts. Gaining strength by going through fire stings and burns. Getting your bark whittled off leaves scars. But those things "will show that your faith is genuine" (1 Peter 1:7). God loves us too much to leave us in our original form. His tools are varied—pain, joy, loss, gain, failure, success—but the outcome is the same. He is whittling away the extra, unnecessary, encumbering stuff to reveal what we were meant to be. Some of us may still end up resembling a pointy stick—but in the hands of the Father, think what a pointy stick can do.

Heavenly Father, thank You for whittling away the things that keep me from being who You created me to be. Please reshape me into Your perfect image of me. Help me let go of the unneeded so I will have room for what is important.

MOLDED PEANUT BUTTER CANDY

While I was growing up, our family received food commodities, including peanut butter in great quantities. We traded some of it, but there was always enough left to make candy!

Ingredients

½ cup creamy peanut butter
3 tablespoons salted butter, softened
1 cup powdered sugar
1 cup semisweet chocolate chips or good-quality melting wafers

Instructions

1. Mix the peanut butter and softened butter together in a mixing bowl. Gradually stir in powdered sugar until fully combined. Cover and place dough in the fridge for about 15 minutes to firm up.
2. While the dough chills, melt the chocolate in a bowl in the microwave for 30 seconds. Stir. Continue microwaving in 15-second increments, stirring well until fully melted.
3. Spoon a little chocolate into each cavity of a hard-plastic chocolate mold* (1-inch-or-smaller cavities work best) so cavities are entirely filled. Wait 1 minute; then flip mold upside down over a piece of waxed paper. Let the excess chocolate drip down onto the paper, leaving each cavity with a thin layer of chocolate coating.
4. Flip the mold again and run a scraper across the top, removing any excess chocolate. Pour excess chocolate from paper back into bowl of chocolate. Refrigerate the mold for 5 or 10 minutes to allow chocolate to harden while working with dough.
5. Remove dough from refrigerator. Using your hands, shape it into small balls. Carefully press one ball into each cavity of your mold, atop the hardened chocolate, filling the cavities ¾ full.
6. Refrigerate at least 20 minutes. Meanwhile, microwave the bowl of chocolate coating in 15-second increments until melted again.
7. Spoon some melted chocolate atop each cavity, spreading it to the edges so peanut butter is completely sealed in. Scrape off excess. Refrigerate mold at least 15 minutes or until chocolate hardens.
8. To serve, remove mold from refrigerator. Let set for 5 minutes. Place a paper towel or dish cloth on the counter. Turn mold over and position over the towel. Tap mold lightly against the towel-covered counter. Candy should come out cleanly, but if not, tap a few more times. Store in an airtight container.
9. *If not using a mold, use a wooden skewer or fork to dip peanut butter shapes into the melted chocolate. Allow excess chocolate to drip off. Place on waxed paper and store in an airtight container.

IT'S A WONDERFUL LIFE

I know how to live on almost nothing or with everything.
I have learned the secret of living in every situation, whether
it is with a full stomach or empty, with plenty or little.

PHILIPPIANS 4:12

Grandma got upset when the grandkids played in the creek.
She worried herself sick when she knew we were swim-
ming, crawdad hunting, or fishing—which in the summer was
nigh on every day. My cousins and I spent massive amounts
of time in the creeks; we just didn't tell Grandma. In summers
that were often hotter than tar on a tin roof, the cold, clear
water was the only thing that kept us cool. On really hot days,
I would take a dip in Gunnit Creek, which bordered my front
yard, then wade across the concrete slab bridge on Brushy
Creek before showing up in her kitchen with water drippin'
down my legs.

Grandma didn't need the creek for cooling down. All she
needed was ice cream. She loved it—especially the homemade
vanilla kind. Suffering with stomach cancer and later Crohn's
disease, I don't think she felt well anytime after 1955. Ice
cream seemed to make her feel better. Somehow it soothed
her. Cooled her.

On most summer weekends, Grandpa would fetch the
ice cream maker from the washhouse and set it just outside
the screened-in side porch. It looked like a wooden bucket or

barrel with a large metal handle attached to a contraption on top. Inside was a tall metal cylinder housing a plastic-coated paddle that fastened to the lid. Its job was to transform everyday ingredients into something otherworldly.

When Grandma whipped up a batch of her vanilla ice cream mix and poured it into the metal cylinder, we would attach the paddle and lid, pack ice and rock salt into the space between the canister and wood, and start cranking. Everyone took turns. Some of us would crank for a minute or so, and others would crank much longer, depending on their gumption and impatience. It seemed to me it took hours and hours and hours. In reality, it took right near half an hour to get a good freeze.

I have clear memories of Uncle Tooter crouched down on his haunches, turning that crank. My uncles were string beans with joints that bent in all kinds of ways most people's don't. When he took his turn, Uncle Tooter would squat down, froglike, with his long, skinny legs looking almost as if they were tied in a bow.

All the cousins in the holler would show up when ice cream was a-churnin'. I guess the crank noises echoed off the trees or something. When it was deemed "froze enough," the men would take apart the ice cream maker and set the frozen cylinder on the porch step. Then Grandma, Mom, or one of the aunts would reach in with a long-handled metal spoon and fill bowls of all shapes and sizes with the brain-freezing ambrosia. Balancing our bowls on our knees, we would sit on the grass or chunks of wood—or if we were really lucky, in one of the few aluminum folding lawn chairs—and thank God for giving us such a wonderful life.

We had very little of what most folks counted as wealth, yet we had more than most. Fresh, clean springs and creeks on hot summer days. A cellar full of canned goods that never seemed to run out. A couple of raggedy lawn chairs. Each other. And homemade ice cream.

We were content.

Today, contentment seems as old-fashioned as hand-powered ice cream makers. We want more, bigger, and better. We want to cram our lives full of grand adventures, global purpose, and great wealth. How many times have you heard phrases like "I want to do something important" or "I want to change the world" from people who don't appreciate the smallest of things?

Maybe going back to the old-fashioned, simple things *is* important and world changing. Teaching our children simple, new skills—or sitting quietly on a summer day listening to the breeze and sharing a bowl of ice cream—can be sacred and purposeful.

We can't let restlessness rob us of contentment. "I have learned how to be content with whatever I have" (Philippians 4:11) is the attitude to strive for. We don't always need more.

Unless it's Grandma's homemade ice cream. Then, definitely, have more.

Lord, thank You for always providing everything I need. When I start to want more or bigger or better, help me be content with what I have—small or large. Remind me again of the simple, free things that bring me joy. Lord, fill my life with gratitude and my heart with love.

GRANDMA'S HOMEMADE ICE CREAM

This recipe was handed from Grandma Dunn to Aunt Joan to me. Aunt Joan still makes it every summer. But her ice cream machine now has an electric motor so her family members don't wear out their arm muscles.

Ingredients
4 eggs
4 cups sugar
2 12-ounce cans of evaporated milk
2 or more tablespoons of vanilla
4–5 quarts of milk

Instructions
1. In a medium bowl, mix together eggs and sugar until sugar starts to dissolve. Whisk in evaporated milk and vanilla.
2. Pour mixture into the cylinder of a 6-quart ice cream maker.
3. Add milk up to the "fill to here" line inside the ice cream maker.
4. Put the paddle and lid in position, attach motor, and turn until ice cream is thick. When it is ready, it will be hard to turn.
5. Top with fruit, caramel, or chocolate syrup if desired.
6. Invite many people over to share the wealth!

Give every day the chance to
become the most beautiful
day of your life.

ATTRIBUTED TO MARK TWAIN

SPRINGS OF WATER

Whoever believes in me, as Scripture has said,
rivers of living water will flow from within them.

JOHN 7:38, NIV

In the forest where I grew up, there were lots of gravel back roads—different from the gravel roads residents used for daily commutes. We didn't travel them all the time, but everyone did at some point, usually during the spring rains when the main roads were flooded. Sometimes, however, we just took a long drive down one of them to see the sights or get away from the everyday.

Along many of these back roads you would see pipes just sticking out of the side of a hill. I'm not sure who installed them or how they chose where to put them. I do know that the pipes tap into springs inside the hills and bring fresh spring water out for passersby to enjoy. Whenever my family drove by one, we stopped, cupped our hands under the pipe, and enjoyed a little refreshment before continuing on our way. Gravel roads are dusty, and a handful of spring water fresh from the rock is the best thirst quencher.

The little church I attended as a kid sits under the shadow of Hawkins Hill. Right there next to the church, one of those pipes still brings spring water from the innards of that hill to thirsty churchgoers. It's pretty near always running. Someone, possibly my Grandpa and his friends, built a concrete basin

for it years ago. The basin was there when my mom attended school at that same little church house, and it is still there. When we have family reunions on the church grounds, we go there to slake our thirst.

But the best spring was at Grandma and Grandpa Dunn's. At one time there was a pipe, like those on the back roads, coming out of the ground between the washhouse and the pond. Eventually, Grandpa and some of my uncles built a small concrete area for the spring to empty into, keeping the water clean so we could easily collect it. But the ducks liked that better than the pond, and they moved the whole family in. So Grandpa and my uncles built a house around the spring to keep the ducks and other varmints out.

A nail right inside the springhouse was where the metal dipper lived. When we cousins wore ourselves out playing tag or hide-and-go-seek, we would race to the springhouse and put dents in the dipper in our determination to grab it first. There were about forty of us cousins, several who lived in the holler around Grandma, so when we had a hankering for a private talk, the springhouse also provided the perfect spot for a sip and quiet conversation.

The springhouse welcomed me when I ran away from home at age eleven because I thought my mom was being completely unfair by denying me something I can't even remember. The peaceful sound of that running water soothed my soul and sent me back home before I was even missed.

My city aunts would go to the springhouse and fill up gallon jugs of water to take back to the city. Nothing tasted so clean and pure. Iced tea made with that water was so much better than any other tea. I didn't realize how good it was until I no longer had access to it.

When the Bible talks about living water, this is the kind of water I think of: Water that is pure and unpolluted. Water that tastes like nothing else. Water I want to run to, drink in, sit beside, and take with me. Water that makes the world a better place. Water that refreshes my soul and changes me from the inside.

Jesus said, "Anyone who believes in me may come and drink!" (John 7:38). That is water I want to drink. And it is the only water that can beat Grandma and Grandpa's spring.

Thank You, Lord, for the refreshment of clean, sweet water, which is easily taken for granted. I appreciate having clean water whenever I need it. But I am even more thankful for Your living water, the water that has washed away my sin and filled me with divine refreshment.

CUCUMBER-INFUSED SPRING WATER

Since most of us are not lucky enough to live where sweet spring water comes out of mountains through a pipe, we have to settle for bottled or tap water. Add some pizzaz to it with this simple recipe.

Ingredients
1 cucumber, sliced
1 lime, sliced
1 bunch of mint, stems trimmed off
Spring water

Instructions
1. Put two slices of cucumber, a slice of lime, and a few sprigs of mint into a 4-ounce glass or a small, deep bowl. Add 2–3 ounces of water. Muddle the ingredients with a straw, fork, or pestle until they have broken apart.
2. Strain the water off the fruit mixture into an 8-ounce glass and top off with more water.
3. Add ice and a decorative lime slice if desired.
4. Alternatively, put all of your ingredients in a glass pitcher filled with spring water and steep overnight. Stir well before serving.

OUTMACGYVERED

Jesus took the five loaves and two fish, looked up toward heaven, and blessed them. Then, breaking the loaves into pieces, he kept giving the bread and fish to the disciples so they could distribute it to the people.

LUKE 9:16

Living right up the hill from Grandma and Grandpa Dunn meant that I skipped down the lane many a morning to check in and see what they were doing. I would often find Grandpa sitting at the kitchen table eating a glassful of corn-bread mush.

One morning I sat beside this tired, humble old man and side-eyed his glass. The question hung between us, though not a word was spoken. At home we often had hot rice with milk and a little bit of sugar and cinnamon mixed in for breakfast. My child brain thought that cornbread and milk would taste similar.

So when Grandpa dug into his glass and held out a spoon-ful for me, I took his offering with gusto. And, Lord have mercy, was it disgusting! It tasted like runny sand. Tears sprang to my eyes. I opened my mouth so my tongue wouldn't touch the goo just behind my teeth. Grandpa slapped his knee, threw back his head, and liked to brought the ceiling down on us with his laughter.

I spat the quicksand-tasting mush into the chicken-feed bucket and ran to the springhouse for a dipper of fresh water to rinse my mouth out. It was the last mush I ever tasted. Ever since then, you can count me out if mush is in the name of a food. That could be why I hate cantaloupe—my family called it mushmelon.

In the summertime, Grandma and Grandpa's massive garden offered up its bounty, including mushmelon. What wasn't eaten was canned. Very little was wasted—peelings and scraps went to the farm animals, and excess fat from butchered animals was rendered into lard that, mixed with a little flour and salt, was transformed into beautiful pie crusts.

Grandma would use it all. She was MacGyver in the kitchen before MacGyver existed. You have biscuits and leftover fried potatoes? That's a lunch sandwich. You have cornbread and milk? That's breakfast cereal.

My grandparents did what they had to do to survive. I am so thankful I came from resourceful people. To this day, I use principles in my home that I learned from them. I open my fridge to see what sort of concoction I can make with whatever ingredients are available, and I can also make a dress out of a tablecloth and turn a basket into a lamp, or vice versa.

That kind of creativity is a gift. It was demonstrated by Jesus and passed along to us. When Jesus needed to feed lunch to a hungry crowd, He didn't ask the disciples to break out the tailgate grills and make a run to the Piggly Wiggly. He used what He had—a few fish and a couple of loaves of bread. "He kept giving the bread and fish to the disciples." He *kept* giving. He turned what was available into enough—with bread left over. (They probably had the leftovers in a bowl of milk the next morning.)

God is still doing that—using what is available. He takes what little we give Him and stretches it into enough. He makes do with our little faith and our piddly prayers. He knits our pain and desperation together into a coat of compassion. He takes our weaknesses and spins them into strength. He out-MacGyvers Grandma.

Father, God, thank You for the creativity You have given me. Lord, transform what I have into enough—with extra left over to bless others. Show me how to be content with what You have provided.

SOUTHERN CORNBREAD

Where I came from, most cooks had self-rising flour in the cupboard at all times. I reckon it's a Southern thing. It didn't last long because we ate a lot of cornbread.

Ingredients

¼ cup bacon grease
1¼ cups self-rising flour
¾ cup yellow cornmeal
½ teaspoon baking soda
1 teaspoon sugar
2 large eggs, lightly beaten
1½ cups buttermilk*

Instructions

1. Preheat oven to 425 degrees. Place bacon grease in a 9-inch cast-iron skillet; heat in oven 5 minutes.
2. While oven is heating, combine flour, cornmeal, baking soda, and sugar; make a well in the center of the mixture.
3. Stir together eggs and buttermilk; add to dry mixture, stirring just until moistened.
4. Carefully remove skillet from oven; tilt skillet to coat bottom and sides with grease. Pour excess hot grease into batter, stir to blend.
5. Pour batter into hot skillet. It should sizzle.
6. Bake for 25 minutes or until golden brown. Let cool 5 minutes. Invert cornbread onto a serving plate; cut into wedges. Serve as a base for pinto beans, or top with honey butter, or offer as bread with any Southern dinner. And if you must, pour milk over the leftovers for breakfast!

* Note: Do not be tempted to substitute milk for the buttermilk. The chemical reaction between the acid in the buttermilk and the soda in the flour makes the bread rise. Add a tablespoon of vinegar to whole milk if you need a substitution.

THE ROOT CELLAR

Let me live forever in your sanctuary,
safe beneath the shelter of your wings!
PSALM 61:4

"It's looking bad to the west!" Grandma's voice crackled over the phone. I took a gander out the window of our trailer, and sure enough, the sky was black and scary.

"Looks like storms are a-comin'!" I said.

"I'm fixin' to head to the cellar. You'uns come on now."

Grandma Dunn was excessively afraid of storms her whole life. She would call to warn us when they were rolling in, and we would run down the lane to join her in the root cellar. It was just up the hill from Grandma's house and just down the hill from ours—close enough to get to if you knew a storm was coming, but far enough that you needed a raincoat or an umbrella if you dillydallied too long. Besides Grandma and Grandpa, three households made use of the root cellar—two of Mom's brothers' families and mine.

My curiosity was always piqued when it came to the cellar. It was off-limits to us kids unless there was a storm. Naturally, "off-limits" meant I had a hankerin' something fierce to get in there.

Years ago, some unknown ancestor dug a space into the hill just beyond the vegetable garden to make the cellar. It sat at the junction of the gravel road—a cow path, really—where it doglegged from Grandma's house to ours. The dark, cool space helped preserve vegetables and seeds that our families put by for the next year's planting.

Its shelves groaned with the weight of the previous year's bounty—row upon row of jars filled with beans, pickles, cabbage, tomatoes, apples, corn, zucchini relish, and more. In the shadowy back of the cellar was a big bin where pounds and pounds of potatoes chilled for the winter. There was a creaky old wood lid on the bin, and during a storm, we cousins would scramble up on it so we could see our parents eye to eye. Their eyes forecasted how bad the storms really were.

Those few times Grandma opened up the cellar to us, I didn't want to miss a thing—the goodies hiding on the shelves, the fullness of the potato bin, the dancing shadows our kerosene lamp would scatter across the walls and ceiling. Even though I knew there was a storm raging outside, I used the opportunity to explore that fantastical place.

Girls with good sense would have hunkered down, minded their manners, and feared the storm. But not being one of those, I examined every canned good, counted the pickles in the jars, and asked a million questions of Grandma as she stood peeking out the door, wringing her hands and watching for a funnel cloud. She also kept an eye on the washhouse, where Grandpa so often whittled away the storm. He was an ornery one.

From the outside, the cellar faded into the trees on the hill, except for cement block arms that welcomed you in. Those blocks existed to keep dirt and water from overtaking the walkway to the door, but to me they looked like arms. Some of my cousins were afraid of the cellar, but I thought of it as a place where the hill reached out to hug us, like a mother hen sheltering her chicks under her wings and close to her heart. I was with the people I loved most, the adults who would protect me with their lives. I was never afraid. I looked forward to storms.

Deuteronomy 33:27 says, "The eternal God is your refuge, and underneath are the everlasting arms" (NIV). That root cellar may have seemed dark and dank to some, but to me, it was the *underneath* arms of refuge. It was safety when home was not.

As an adult, I forget the opportunities storms bring. In the root cellar our blessings were right there on the shelves to be counted. We were surrounded by the people we loved, and God's protection felt as real as the cinder blocks holding up the shelves.

Storms redirect our focus. They help us reconnect to our faith. Storms teach us how to weather the calms.

We rode out many a storm in that cellar. Not once did we see a funnel, nor did we lose any property. But in that cellar, our family's roots grew deeper. It truly was a root cellar.

Dear God, You are my refuge and strength. Thank You for being the shelter I can always run to. Lord, thank You also for the storms that have deepened my roots and built my trust in You. Let those roots be enough to get me through the sunny days when I tend to forget how close You really are.

GRANDMA'S ZUCCHINI RELISH

I believe this is the recipe used in the jars of relish that adorned Grandma's root cellar. None of us seem to know where this recipe originated, but lots of my aunts and cousins on both sides of the family can pints of it each year. We use it in salads, on hot dogs, or as a side dish.

Ingredients

10 cups zucchini, grated

4 cups onion, finely diced

3 cups carrots, shredded

2 cups bell pepper, finely diced

¼ cup canning salt

2 cups vinegar

4 cups sugar

2 tablespoons cornstarch mixed with 2 tablespoons water

2 teaspoons celery seed

1 teaspoon black pepper

1 teaspoon turmeric

1 teaspoon nutmeg

Instructions

1. Combine zucchini, onion, carrots, peppers, and salt. Let stand in the refrigerator for at least 3 hours or overnight.
2. Drain vegetable mixture.
3. Combine vinegar, sugar, cornstarch mixture, celery seed, black pepper, turmeric, and nutmeg in a large pot. Bring to a boil.
4. Add vegetables.
5. Bring to a boil again. Reduce heat and simmer for 15 minutes.
6. Wash 6 or 7 pint-sized canning jars and lids. Place jars in hot water to heat up.
7. Pour mixture into hot jars and seal lids onto jars. Place jars in large pot and process in boiling water bath (212 degrees) for 10 minutes.
8. Remove jars from water bath with tongs and set on counter to cool. You will hear a pop as the jars cool off and the lids seal.
9. Tighten rings and let cool completely. Makes 6–7 pints of relish.

To "put by" is an old, deep-country way of saying to "save something you don't use now, against the time when you'll need it."

RUTH HERTZBERG,
Putting Food By

BEANS AND CORNBREAD

*Joseph opened up the storehouses and distributed
grain to the Egyptians, for the famine was
severe throughout the land of Egypt.*

GENESIS 41:56

Interwoven with the memories of Grandma's kitchen is a
soundtrack of spewing, shushing, *chicka-chicka-chicka*
noises from the pressure cooker. Sometimes chicken was stew-
ing in preparation for dumplins. But mostly the jiggling top
spewed the aroma of pinto beans.

Beans and cornbread ruled Grandma's menu. They were
cheap and easy and went a long way to feed a big family.
Grandma Dunn gave birth to fourteen kids, including three sets
of twins. Their family needed cheap and easy.

They lived in our small valley tucked away in its forest.
Grandma had operated a small country store passed down
from her parents and grandparents—until blacktop roads
became a thing and traffic stopped comin' around our mountain in favor of roller-coastering over it. Money, historically
tight, dried up after the store closed. But the family farm—
across the creek from the store—and cheap, dried beans saved
the family.

Dried beans and cornmeal could be stored in the cellar,
smokehouse, or deep freeze for long periods of time—up to a
year or two as long as they stayed dry and bug-free. Add some

potatoes from the cellar bins, and you had a meal right near perfect for hillbilly families—beans served both as the main course and a side dish. One pot fed all the young'uns. They were ever present.

The habit of storing beans and cornmeal was not something Grandma passed on to my mom. Mom stored tons of potatoes, kraut, and pickles, but never beans. She didn't like beans. My stepdad, Everett, however, loved them. So he and I, along with my brothers, Mike and Virgil, would mosey on down to Grandma's for a bowl whenever we got a hankerin'. Her store never failed us. Because of Grandma's foresight, our bean cravings were always satisfied.

Grandma stored what was essential when we didn't. She put up vegetables, fruit, and lard against an unknown future. She had chickens and potato bins and frozen necessities of all kinds. Her nature was to lay aside in abundance what would be needed in scarcity.

She had Joseph's wisdom.

One of Jacob's twelve sons, Joseph, miraculously overcame being sold into slavery by his brothers to become the second highest official in Egypt. "Pharaoh put Joseph in charge of all Egypt" (Genesis 41:43).

Joseph's rise was God-ordained. God had let him know that a drought was a-comin' when he interpreted a couple of Pharaoh's dreams; seven years of plenty would be followed by seven years of famine.

Joseph prepared. He had storage barns built and filled them with the excess each year. When the famine finally came, "people from all around came to Egypt to buy grain from

Joseph because the famine was severe throughout the world" (Genesis 41:57). Joseph's wisdom saved a nation—and his own family.

That kind of foresight is not something all of us possess. Grandma did. Beans and cornbread may not compare to silos of wheat and grain, but her planning saved her family through many lean years. The wisdom of being prepared can be adopted by anyone.

Lord, thank You for giving wisdom to the people who care for me. Please give me the kind of foresight and planning I need to be a resource for others. When I have plenty, help me to remember to store it for those who have less, even if it is simply a bowl of beans and cornbread.

LEFTOVER PINTO DIP

When I had sleepovers at my cousin Lynn's house, there was *always* beans and cornbread. Her mom had learned beans-and-cornbread cooking from Grandma Dunn and made them daily. We would sneak out of Lynn's room in the middle of the night and have a bowl of leftover beans with dill pickles and cornbread. That's a good option for enjoying beans, but for something a little different, try this spread. It's good on toasted cornbread and baguettes and is also tasty with vegetable sticks.

Ingredients

1 clove garlic, peeled
Kosher salt
1 cup leftover cooked pinto beans
Freshly ground black pepper
1 tablespoon apple cider vinegar
½ cup tomatoes, finely diced
1 cup crumbled feta or goat cheese, or grated cheddar
2 tablespoons olive oil
¼ cup minced fresh basil or dill or other herb

Instructions

1. Finely mince the garlic. Sprinkle it with a generous amount of salt and mash into a paste.
2. Rinse beans. Combine the beans and garlic paste with a few grinds of pepper and the vinegar. Set aside for 30 minutes to marinate.
3. Place the tomatoes, cheese, and olive oil in a bowl and stir to combine thoroughly. Pour vinegar/bean mixture over tomato mixture. Refrigerate for a few hours to allow the flavors to blend and the tomatoes to release their juice. Then bring to room temperature.
4. Add the herbs, stir, and transfer to the vessel of your choice. Serve with vegetable sticks, or spread on toasted bread or leftover cornbread.

RIPE PERSIMMONS

Solid food belongs to those who are of full age,
that is, those who by reason of use have their
senses exercised to discern both good and evil.

HEBREWS 5:14, NKJV

Between Grandma's house and ours, alongside a gravel lane that snuggles up to a foothill in the Mark Twain National Forest, grew a persimmon tree. When I was a young girl, I passed this tree every day. Indistinct from its neighbors in the summer, it was spectacular in the golden changing time of autumn. The plumlike fruits turned yellowy-orange and bobbed in the breeze, taunting me to pluck them. But I knew better than to eat them early. I would wait until the tree released the persimmons from its branches. Then, and only then, I would grab one on my way to or from Grandma's. Those persimmons were sweet and sticky and seemed to glow from the inside out. I sometimes took more than one—and I never ate a persimmon without intentionally cracking open one of its seeds.

The technique is akin to opening a sunflower seed: Get the seam of the shell lined up between your teeth and bite down. When you do it right, the shell will split clean in half. Then you simply spit out the two halves to inspect the kernel.

Folklore says that if the kernel inside is spoon-shaped, expect lots of heavy, wet snow to fall before winter is over. If the kernel is fork-shaped, expect a mild winter. If the kernel is knife-shaped, expect cutting, icy winds.

My family has been followers of the persimmon school of meteorology since before I was born. Many of them still are. It is surprisingly accurate. According to the University of Missouri Jefferson City Extension Office, which collected persimmon seeds from across the country for years to test this theory, persimmon seeds were correct fifteen out of the nineteen years examined.

Persimmons are notoriously bitter before they ripen. Biting into one will put a pucker on your face and an ache in your belly. Even the deer leave them alone. The sour fruit has small, undeveloped seeds that are worthless weather predictors until the fruit is ripe and falling off the trees. The impatient pull beautiful, orange, pre-ripe orbs off the tree and are disappointed. Only mature seeds can open up about the future; the signs simply aren't there before then.

Getting an accurate weather forecast is just the beginning. The ripened fruit are perfect for jellies, puddings, and salads, and they actually make a great addition to a charcuterie board—for those highfalutin folks.

Waiting may be hard. Seeing that fruit hanging there every day as I skipped up the lane was torture. But I knew eating it prematurely would give me a tummy ache and make my eyes squinch up. Waiting is worth it.

One of the pivotal stories in the Old Testament is a story of waiting . . . and not waiting. God promised Abraham that he and his wife, Sarah, would have millions of descendants. But these two were older than dirt. As much as Sarah wanted to believe God's promise, she couldn't believe in her own body. She was years beyond childbearing age. Rather than waiting for the promise to come to fruition, Sarah gave her maid to her husband so she could have a baby instead. Sarah ate the sour persimmon, and her life was bitter for a long time.

God was faithful, however, and eventually blessed ninety-year-old Sarah with a baby who became the father of the nation of Israel. Her disbelief in her biological systems didn't change God's promise. But what if she had waited? What if she hadn't eaten the bitter fruit of impatience? How would her life have been different? How can ours be sweeter if we wait for maturity instead of acting rashly? Bitter or sweet, the choice is ours.

Lord, help me find the sweetness in waiting. I want to mature and act at just the right time. If I am getting impatient, please remind me how bitter rushing things can be.

LEAF LETTUCE WITH PERSIMMONS

We made salads like this using fresh leaf lettuce from the garden or watercress from the creek. But with radicchio and arugula so easily accessible these days, you can substitute what works best for you.

Ingredients

Dressing
¼ cup extra-virgin olive oil
3 tablespoons red wine vinegar
1 teaspoon honey mustard
3 teaspoons sugar
½ teaspoon coarse salt

Salad
1 pound mixed lettuces, such as watercress, radicchio, frisée, arugula, or leaf lettuce, torn into 1-inch pieces (9 cups)
½ cup walnuts, toasted and coarsely chopped
3 persimmons, peeled and cut into half-inch wedges
½ cup pomegranate seeds, berries, cranberries, or grapes
Coarse salt and freshly ground pepper

Instructions

1. Gradually whisk oil into vinegar and mustard in a small bowl until well mixed. Stir in sugar and salt.
2. Toss lettuces, walnuts, persimmons, and pomegranate seeds (or berries or grapes) in a large bowl. Add the dressing and toss to coat. Season with salt and pepper.

Persimmons will all get fit
to eat, and the nuts will
be dropping like rain all
through the woods here.

EUDORA WELTY, *The Wide Net*

CORNY

*I will take out your stony, stubborn heart
and give you a tender, responsive heart.*

EZEKIEL 36:26

Late summers saw the harvesting of Grandma and Grandpa's corn that grew in the field between their barn and our home up the hill. They didn't plant enough to need a combine or fancy equipment—just lots of handpicking and tossing in baskets.

Every summer we sat outside Grandma and Grandpa's house on benches and old wooden chairs under the shade of a huge oak tree and shucked what seemed like a million ears. Aunts, uncles, and cousins would come to help. We would catch up on the latest news and jokes while tossing corn left and right. On breaks, some of us would grab an icy bottle of soda from a big galvanized tub, put one foot up on the fence, and commence to jawing about the size of the harvest, garden pests, and other topics.

As best as I can recollect, there were two kinds of corn. The yellow eating corn was fried, frozen, or canned. The white field corn was made into hominy or used to feed the livestock.

Grandma turned the yellow corn into a fried masterpiece. She would cut the kernels off the cob into a huge skillet, then scrape the milk out of the cob over the corn, add a little sugar, and let it caramelize into mouthwatering lusciousness. If you have never smelled corn frying in a bath of bacon grease and butter, you have missed out. Served up with some fried rabbit and sliced tomatoes . . . well, let's just say a few uncles got wooed into the family with this meal.

Field corn is harder than sweet corn. Cornflakes and cattle feed are made from it. If you were to eat it fresh off the stalk, it could break every tooth in your head. Harvested later than sweet corn, it must be processed for human consumption. To get the hard hull off and the corn softened up, we would boil it in the big maple syrup kettle with a few scoops of lye. Farmers use lye for all kinds of things. Farmers' wives use it for making soap and hominy.

Now lye, otherwise known as sodium hydroxide, is dangerous. It can cause burns on skin and, if handled incorrectly, flame up. The component that makes lye dangerous, however, also puffs the corn and softens the kernel. Without going through a lye bath, feed corn is just feed corn.

If you want hominy, you have to brave the danger. Grandma and Grandpa dried their corn, then pulled the kernels from the cobs and boiled them in lye until the hulls came off. I wasn't allowed anywhere near it—which goes to show the deep intelligence of my kinfolk! Once the corn was thoroughly rinsed and put back in the kettle to boil for a couple of hours, you couldn't bribe me away. I had to see the corn newly puffed and twice the size it was before.

When the boiling was finished, Grandma, Mom, and the aunts canned or froze the corn. Grits and masa, the main ingredient in tortillas and tamales, are made from dried hominy. But we didn't grow up with grits or tortillas—we ate plain ole hominy heated up with a little bacon fat. Years later I discovered ways to elevate our humble hominy into soups, casseroles, and cheesy side dishes. Be it ever so humble, there is no corn like hominy.

Spiritually, our hearts are prone to be a bit like field corn—hard and tough. To soften them up, God sometimes puts us in hot water or through some danger. We have to lose our hard outer shells before our hearts are soft enough to be usable. God promises in Ezekiel that He will "take out your stony, stubborn heart and give you a tender, responsive heart" (36:26). That is what I want: a soft, tender heart.

And a bowl of steaming hominy soup.

Lord, I desire a tender heart. Take away any hardness that keeps me from being palatable to those who need me. Thank You for loving me enough to soften my heart to the things that matter to You.

HOMINY SOUP

This is not a soup I had growing up, but it has come to be one of my favorites. This version takes no time to put together and uses easy-to-find ingredients. It is also a great way to use the leftover chicken from Grandma Dunn's Chicken and Dumplins recipe if needed.

Ingredients

1 can hominy (29 ounces)
4–6 cups chicken or vegetable broth
1 tablespoon vegetable oil
1 medium onion, chopped
4 cloves garlic, minced
½ rotisserie chicken, shredded, bones and skin removed (or the left-over chicken from Grandma Dunn's Chicken and Dumplins recipe)
½ teaspoon cumin
1 teaspoon oregano
1 cup crushed tomatoes
2 whole chipotle peppers in adobo sauce, chopped
Juice from a lime
Fresh cilantro for garnish

Optional
Shredded cabbage, thin radish slices, cotija cheese, or other garnishes

Instructions

1. Drain the water from the can of hominy and place hominy in a medium saucepan. Add 4 cups chicken broth to saucepan and bring to a boil.
2. Turn heat to low and simmer for 15 minutes.
3. While the hominy is simmering, add the oil to a large stockpot over medium heat.
4. Add chopped onion to the pan and cook until translucent. Add more oil if necessary.
5. Stir the garlic into the onion and cook for another minute.
6. Add the shredded chicken, cumin, oregano, and crushed tomatoes.
7. Stir in the chopped chipotle peppers in adobo sauce, along with hominy and broth.
8. Bring the soup to a boil, then reduce the heat to low and let simmer for 30 minutes. If it gets too thick, add more chicken stock.
9. Ladle into bowls and add a splash of lime juice and fresh cilantro to each bowl. Serve with garnishes of your choice; shredded cabbage, thin radish slices, and cotija cheese are traditional.

UNWANTED KISSES

Jesus said, "Judas, would you betray
the Son of Man with a kiss?"
LUKE 22:48

Vincent kept eyeing me. From seeing him practicing his pucker all day, I knew he wanted to kiss me, and my nine-year-old brain thought that was beyond disgusting. I would rather get a kiss from Grandpa's whiskery, slobbery old mule. Yeah, he was my aunt's nephew by marriage, and, being the same age, we played in Grandma's yard together when he visited every summer, but I still thought he was meaner than a hound dog with a toothache.

I decided I would outsmart the rascal, so I doubled back into Grandma's kitchen to hide out and get some Watkins flavored water. I was leaning against the kitchen counter, basking in my superior intellect and evasion skills, when a pair of lips seemed to materialize out of thin air, plunking a smelly, wet kiss smack-dab on my left ear.

I took off like a firecracker. My aunt had just gone out the storm door, and I tried to catch it before it closed. I was a second too late. I was running so fast that I went plumb through the glass and landed upside down with one arm draped across the broken glass.

There was no blood, but my arm was cut clean to the bone. I was so busy getting right side up to make sure Vincent wasn't tryin' to kiss me again that I didn't realize what had happened—until my mom saw the cut. Then the shoutin' started. There was wailin' and cryin', and not all of it was from me.

Uncle Jack grabbed me and tossed me into Grandpa's blue pickup truck and drove me and Mom, both barefooted, the thirty miles to the hospital. I was held down, poked, sewed, and made right as rain relatively quickly. Nurses and orderlies may have been injured in the process. I was a very strong little hillbilly.

A few days later, as I lay on Grandma's couch milking my nineteen-stitches injury for all it was worth, Vincent came to see if I was okay. He brought flowers. They were picked from Grandma's yard, but they were flowers all the same, and flowers can't be ignored. It made me spittin' mad to admit that he wasn't half bad—after all, I really hadn't wanted his kiss that turned me upside down.

I wonder how Jesus felt knowing He would receive a kiss that would turn *His* world upside down. Even though Judas had far darker motives than Vincent, and Jesus knew what that kiss would mean, He didn't hide from it. He didn't run headlong through a door. Instead, He prayed about it—"My Father, if it is not possible for this cup to be taken away unless I drink it, may your will be done" (Matthew 26:42, NIV).

It hadn't occurred to me to pray. Running seemed the best option. Yet running from difficulties can turn your world upside down and bring suffering. It can even run up your hospital bill.

Face the issue instead: Talk. Pray. Trust.

You can always trust God. He's not like Vincent. Vincent was pretty sneaky . . .

Heavenly Father, thank You for your protection and comfort when my world seems upside down. You know what it is like to want to evade a situation with all Your being. You know what it is to face it head on. With compassion, You right my world. Give me the strength to face whatever comes my way.

PINEAPPLE UPSIDE-DOWN CAKE

Grandma Dunn's recipe for this cake has been lost. An easy alternative is to make the topping but use a regular yellow cake mix, substituting pineapple juice for the water. You can trust me on that.

Ingredients

Topping

⅓ cup butter
½ cup brown sugar, packed
10–12 pineapple rings, patted dry with paper towels
Maraschino cherries

Vanilla Cake

½ cup mayonnaise (I use Duke's)
¾ cup sugar
2 eggs, room temperature
2 teaspoons vanilla
1½ cups flour
1½ teaspoons baking powder
½ teaspoon salt
½ cup pineapple juice (from can; add water if needed to make ½ cup)

Instructions

1. Preheat oven to 350 degrees.
2. Put butter in a 10-inch cake pan. Place in oven until butter is melted—about 4–5 minutes.
3. Remove from oven and brush melted butter up the sides of the pan.
4. Evenly sprinkle brown sugar over melted butter.
5. Starting in the center of the pan, arrange pineapple slices over sugar to cover the bottom of the pan. Cut remaining slices in half and stand up against the sides of the pan.
6. Place cherries in the center of the pineapple rings. Let cool.
7. For cake batter, mix mayonnaise, sugar, and eggs with a hand mixer until well blended. Stir in vanilla.
8. Combine flour, baking powder, and salt in separate bowl.
9. Alternate adding flour mixture and pineapple juice to batter, mixing with a spoon just until combined. Do not overmix.
10. Carefully pour batter evenly over pineapple/cherries.
11. Bake for 30 minutes. Check cake and cover with foil if the top is getting too brown. Bake another 15 minutes, until a toothpick inserted in the center comes out mostly clean.
12. Cool for about 12 minutes before inverting cake onto a plate. Remove cake pan. Serve warm with a scoop of ice cream.

A LITTLE BIRDIE TOLD ME

A bird in the sky may carry your words,
and a bird on the wing may report what you say.
ECCLESIASTES 10:20, NIV

When I was growing up, talking on the telephone meant taking turns with two or three other families who were on the same party line. We shared a line with Grandma and Grandpa and the Ribbles. It was not unusual to pick up the phone and catch people midconversation.

"Well, I heard a tornado touched down in Hogan."

"Lord have mercy, is everyone all right?"

You never knew what you might intrude upon. Mostly it was just the dial tone. But sometimes secrets were being discussed. One time I picked up to hear, " . . . Marilyn's surprise birthday party."

I hung up quickly. *I'll swan! I didn't want to know that.*

After words get beyond our teeth, they are no longer ours. On a party line, the chance of eavesdropping was fairly high. Thankfully the other people on our line weren't big talkers or listeners. They didn't have much use for a phone, which meant more privacy for us.

All the houses in our area were on shared party lines. So even if my party didn't have eavesdroppers, the girls I called shared lines with some of the biggest blabbers in the area. If there was anything that needed to be kept secret, the phone was not the place to discuss it.

Grandma's kitchen was like a less-public party line. Lots of information flowed while we were peeling potatoes, washing dishes, or canning vegetables. If you wanted to know what was happening in the family, all you had to do was listen.

It's amazing how many family secrets are whispered in front of kids. Adults think kids aren't listening or don't understand. That may be true in certain situations—but corn ain't the only thing that has ears!

Besides the secret to a good chocolate pie, I found out about much family drama in Grandma's kitchen: Grandpa's travels, suspicious fires, which aunts were not speaking to which cousins, and uncertain parentage. Recently some cousins and I were discussing family secrets—how we knew them, when we learned them. We looked at each other and said, "We just knew." Secrets were soaked up in the kitchen like we sopped up gravy with a biscuit.

Some secrets, however, didn't stay in the kitchen. Bits of information would break off and leak onto innocent bystanders. I'm pretty sure that's how people knew Grandpa was a jailbird. As much as the family would have preferred secrecy, the whole blamed county knew.

In the hollers, everyone did controlled burns in the springtime to prepare fields for planting. Still do as far as I know. Once when a good-sized chunk of the National Forest caught fire, someone accused Grandpa's burn. The whispers spread through the holler like, well, wildfire.

Grandpa swore it wasn't him. But a few days after the fire,

he went to jail just the same. The news leaked out that he had been burning a field near the time of the forest fire. No one knew how that information spread. It must have been a little birdie.

That little birdie has apparently been around for centuries. "A bird in the sky may carry your words, and a bird on the wing may report what you say" (Ecclesiastes 10:20, NIV). Thousands of years before party lines existed, one Old Testament writer understood how easily words leak out.

The solution is simple: Keep those secret words behind your teeth. If birds don't hear them, they can't take flight.

Heavenly Father, thank You for guarding my words. Help me be a trusted information keeper. When the urge bubbles up to share secrets, help me to keep the words safe behind my teeth.

CHICKEN PUFFS

The filling in these chicken puffs, like words, sometimes leaks out, so make sure they are completely sealed. Even though it is a bit fancy, it is not expensive to create. And it makes an impression.

Ingredients

½ cup onion, chopped
3 tablespoons butter, divided
Small bag (8–10 ounces) fresh spinach, chopped
15 ounces ricotta or cottage cheese
2 tablespoons fresh parsley, chopped
2 teaspoons fresh basil, chopped
1 teaspoon oregano
1 egg
Salt and pepper
1 package (8 ounces) sliced mushrooms
1 pound boneless, skinless chicken breasts, cut in bite-sized pieces
2 cans crescent-dough sheets (or 2 cans crescent rolls)

Instructions

1. Preheat oven to 375 degrees. Line two large (18 x 13) rimmed baking sheets with parchment paper or silicone mats.
2. In a skillet, sauté onions in 1 tablespoon butter until soft. Mix in chopped spinach and stir until wilted. Remove from heat.
3. In a medium bowl, mix ricotta, parsley, basil, oregano, egg, salt, and pepper. Add spinach mixture. Set aside.
4. Add 1 tablespoon butter to skillet and sauté mushrooms with a little salt and pepper until slightly browned. Remove from pan and set aside to cool.
5. Add last tablespoon of butter to pan and lightly salt chicken pieces. Sauté chicken until no longer pink. Remove from pan and set aside to cool.
6. Divide each dough sheet into 4 equal pieces. (If using crescent rolls, pinch together 2 triangles to make a rectangle; seal well.) Place an equal portion of chicken in the center of each of the 8 pieces of dough.
7. Top chicken with spinach mixture and then mushrooms, dividing equally.
8. Wrap dough up and over to seal all the chicken and veggies completely inside dough. Place on baking sheets. Bake for about 12 minutes or until golden brown. Makes 8 puffs.

The tongue is a small member,
yet it boasts of great things.
How great a forest is set
ablaze by such a small fire!

JAMES 3:5, ESV

THE BEAUTY WITHIN

The LORD does not look at the things people look at.
People look at the outward appearance,
but the LORD looks at the heart.
1 SAMUEL 16:7, NIV

The bottomland between Brushy Creek and Grandpa's barn was home to a little grove of maple trees. Every fall they seemed to have a competition to outdo each other with color: butter, lemon, flame, crimson, sienna, rose, magenta, umber, scarlet. Then the sunlight would shift, and their colors would rearrange into a new breathtaking palette. Romance stories are written with trees such as these as backdrops.

Grandpa and my parents, uncles, and brothers tapped the maples in springtime to take advantage of their sweet sap. They drilled a small hole into each tree, stuck a metal spigot into the hole, and hung a bucket or plastic milk jug on the spigot. Clear, sweet sap dripped into the buckets with a regular *tap, tap, tap*. Cold nights and warmer days kept the sap flowing for weeks, and we gathered the liquid until it filled a huge black kettle. Then the menfolk hung the kettle on a sturdy metal hook and built a raging fire underneath it right outside the barnyard.

Next the boiling began. The men took turns maintaining the kettle for twelve to fourteen hours, feeding the fire and stirring the pot until clear sap transformed into golden syrup.

The fire drew people. Neighbors would come lean against the wooden fence or the metal gate and jaw on about coon hunting or crops or whatever news was worth repeating. Some squatted next to the fire for warmth or pulled up a tree stump to sit on. It was, after all, the most exciting thing happening in the holler. Stories were swapped, advice given, and breezes shot. Even the cows came over, stuck their noses through the fence, and offered a mooed exhortation.

Once the sap had concentrated down to a more manageable volume, the still-thin liquid was strained and taken inside for the womenfolk to finish off. Grandma boiled it until the sap was thick, beautiful sweetness. We poured it into hot mason jars, then stood them upside down for a minute or two before flipping them upright to wait on the *plink* sound that meant the jars were sealed.

It takes about forty gallons of sap to make a gallon of syrup. Grandpa's trees had enough for each of our families to have syrup on hand until the next year's gathering. Mopping up a puddle of that syrup with one of Mom's pancakes was truly a beautiful thing.

The sugar maples have both an obvious and a hidden beauty. Their fall colors are their crowning glory. But beneath their ordinary bark, deep within the heart of the tree when it's bare-branched and lifeless looking, lives sap that, when nurtured and developed, gives the leaves a run for their money in the beauty and wonder department.

Beauty like that was also found in Esther. She was a woman who "was admired by everyone who saw her" (Esther 2:15). She drew admirers like flies to maple syrup.

Her outer beauty brought her the attention of the king, and her inner beauty saved her nation.

Esther would not have had the opportunity to meet a king, much less inspire him to change the world, had she not been beautiful on the outside. He was looking for someone who would delight his eye, but he made her queen because she was so much more than lovely. She was respectful, polite, humble, generous, and selfless.

Because of her outer beauty, her inner beauty found a place to shine. The king loved and respected her. He saw her heart.

What is your inner self like? Is it still in the sap form, or has it developed into a deep sweetness? Keep the fire going until the beauty inside matches the potential that God already sees. It's there waiting to shine.

Father, thank You for the beauty within me, even when it's hidden. Take the raw materials of my life and boil them down into a sweet soul that is fit for the King of kings.

MAPLE-COATED BACON

Many people refer to this type of bacon as Million Dollar Bacon. It doesn't cost a million dollars to make, thank the Lord, but bacon dressed in a shiny maple coat is definitely beautiful inside and out.

Ingredients

1 pound thick-cut bacon
3 tablespoons maple syrup
¼ cup packed brown sugar
Black pepper

Instructions

1. Position oven rack in middle of oven. Preheat oven to 350 degrees.
2. Cover a baking sheet in foil. Place a wire baking rack on the pan.
3. In a small bowl, mix maple syrup and brown sugar into a thick paste. Rub a little mix on each side of the bacon and lay flat in a single layer on wire rack.
4. Bake in center of oven for 20 minutes. Remove and carefully turn bacon over. Bake for another 15–20 minutes. It should be slightly dark (not burnt) and crispy. If not, cook in 2-minute increments until done.
5. Remove from oven and let cool on rack. After 4–5 minutes, place bacon slices on parchment paper. The sugar is very hot (be careful) and will harden after a few minutes, making the bacon stick to the rack if not removed. Serve at room temperature. Serves 4–5.

Part 2

COME SIT A SPELL AT MOM'S

Mama had a way of making us
feel good about everything.
DOLLY PARTON

EVERLASTING COMMODITIES

"What can I do to help you?" Elisha asked [the widow].
"Tell me, what do you have in the house?" "Nothing at all,
except a flask of olive oil," she replied.
2 KINGS 4:2

When I was growing up, my stepfather, Everett, lost his business when a five-story scaffold failed and dropped him and his four brothers to the ground. All were injured, he the most severely. That's when we moved to the country, just down the holler from Grandma and Grandpa, so he could heal and we could figure out this new life.

Part of that meant living under the poverty level and receiving commodities like enormous blocks of cheese, large cans of peanut butter, and family-sized packages of macaroni and potato flakes, among other things. Thus began my adventures in the kitchen.

What do you make with a sixteen-ounce box of potato flakes when you have a cellar full of real potatoes you've grown in your garden? I mean, we had fried potatoes almost daily. What good were fake spuds?

It turns out they made excellent donuts.

A can of tomato juice paired with a can of chicken also made a decent chicken chili. Many days I opened the cabinets, took a survey of what was available, and came up with some new concoction not found in any cookbook. Often it was really,

really good. Sometimes it was very, very bad. We don't speak of those meals. With each experiment, I learned something about food combinations, cooking, and how to make do with what you have.

Mostly I learned that no matter what was going on, God provided what we needed to survive. The cabinets were never completely bare, even if composing a meal from what we had on hand did require imaginative thinking.

So many people panic and run to the store to buy massive quantities of food and household goods when a hurricane is predicted or a snowstorm threatens or a power outage or pandemic upends normal life. I look in my well-stocked pantry and fridge and think, *Hmmm, I bet I can make really cool new recipes with this stuff. I've done it before; I can do it again. On the shelf is harissa and cod, hominy and sausage? No need to panic. God has always provided. He will again.*

I trust Him because I have been in a place where trusting Him was all that stood between our family and starvation.

In 2 Kings 4:1-7, the story of the widow who was down to her last bit of oil reminds me just how much I can trust God. His timing may not be my timing (no one wants to be on their last bag of ramen before being able to restock), but He always has an answer. Afraid that her sons would be sold into slavery to pay her debts, the only thing the widow could do was ask for help. She knew Elisha was tight with God, so she asked him. Through Elisha's instructions, God answered. He kept her small flask pouring more and more oil until every vessel her sons could find was full.

The coolest thing about this story is that God has repeated

it over and over. Stories about His provision have been passed down since the beginning of recorded time. He pours out answers if we ask, and if we provide vessels for Him to fill. That's the key: Ask and have an empty vessel ready.

Whatever we're facing—pandemics, aging parents, economic hardship, a two-year-old's tantrum—God has what we need. Ask Him to fill you. Open your soul to Him so He can pour into it. If His provision includes potato flakes, I have a recipe for that!

Heavenly Father, thank You for providing everything I need. Thank You for being with me through plenty and through scarcity. Help me to empty myself of worries and anxieties so I have room for Your love and provision. Pour into me all I need to make it through this day, this week, this month. I trust You with all that I have.

HOMEMADE POTATO-FLAKE DONUTS

Originally we made this recipe with powdered milk since we had huge boxes of it alongside the potato flakes in the pantry. If you have some, try using ⅔ cup of the powder, and change the milk to water.

Ingredients

½ cup butter, melted
¾ cup sugar
1½ teaspoons salt
1 cup instant potato flakes
2½ cups warm whole milk, 110–115 degrees
1 tablespoon yeast
2 eggs, beaten
5–5½ cups flour
Cooking oil

Instructions

1. In a large bowl, with a large spoon, mix together butter, sugar, salt, and potato flakes. Pour in warm milk. Sprinkle yeast over top and allow to get foamy. Stir in beaten eggs a little at a time so they don't cook in the warm milk. With a Danish whisk or using your hands, mix in 5 cups of flour, adding more as needed to make a stiff dough.
2. Cover bowl with a clean towel and let rise until doubled in size, about an hour.
3. On a well-floured surface, roll out the dough until it's about a half-inch thick. With a donut cutter or a glass, cut out the donuts, using a cap from a vanilla bottle or something similar to cut out the centers.
4. Cover with towel and let dough rise again for about 45 minutes.
5. Fill a pan about 2 inches deep with cooking oil and heat it to 375 degrees. The oil is hot enough when a small amount of dough (such as a donut hole) floats and browns in about 60 seconds.
6. Fry 2 or 3 donuts at a time for about 60 seconds on each side. Don't crowd the pan. Test the first donut to make sure it cooks through. Oil that is too hot will produce doughy insides, while temperatures that are too low produce greasy donuts.
7. When the donut is golden on both sides, take it out with tongs or chopsticks and allow the excess oil to drain back into the pan. Place the donut on a plate lined with several layers of paper towels.
8. Roll cooled donuts in powdered sugar or cinnamon and sugar, or fully submerge in Aunt Joan's Chocolate Icing (see page 155).

He satisfies the thirsty
and fills the hungry
with good things.

PSALM 107:9

TABLES

Moses placed the table in the tent of meeting
on the north side of the tabernacle outside the curtain
and set out the bread on it before the LORD.
EXODUS 40:22–23, NIV

Living five miles down a gravel road that crossed two creeks deep in the forest meant entertainment was relegated to playing games with people who also lived in the boonies . . . and were related to me directly, or at least once or twice removed. We were big on card and board games: Monopoly, spoons, Trivial Pursuit, Rook, rummy, the occasional game of toothpick poker. These games were played at the rickety kitchen table, where we sat on even more rickety wooden chairs.

Conversation flowed in waves: "Is the cabbage ready to can?" "Did you hear that someone was picked up for streaking through the campground up the holler?" "Have you weaned the piglets yet?" We played hard and laughed harder.

On one game night, as the family sat around the table, the hand just dealt, Mom held her cards close to her face just in case anyone was figurin' on cheatin'. While still organizing the cards in our hands, we heard a loud pop. Mom began sinking, little by little. The stunned look in her eyes was hilarious. The further she sank, the more tightly she gripped her cards. Her wide eyes reflected disbelief and confusion.

Then, with another loud pop, shaky chair legs gave way and

inelegantly dumped Mom onto the floor. We watched, amazed, as she sprang up from the floor with her cards held close to her chest, looked around the table, and said, "No one saw my cards, did they?"

We laughed until we cried. Her pride and behind were a bit bruised, so we procured another chair—with a padded cushion—and continued to play around the table.

The truth is, that creaky table was the family member we leaned on most. It caught our tears when we sobbed after funerals and guarded our sweet tea while we whispered behind-our-hand secrets. It supported the weight of hogs being butchered, multitiered wedding cakes, and dozens upon dozens of jars of vegetables being put up for the winter. Adorned with biscuits and breads, it welcomed friends and strangers. Laughter echoed off its scuffed top. Strategy was plotted around its circumference. And frustration reverberated across the wood from the slaps of angry hands.

If tables could talk . . .

God told Moses to build a table—for the Tabernacle that traveled across the wilderness with the Israelites. It held the bread offered to the Lord and stood near the altar where sacrifices were made, not far from the curtain that separated the "Holy of Holies," where God's presence dwelt.

Imagine what that table could have told us—stories of dedication and faith, misdirection and failings, dark and light, the presence of God. The table of the Tabernacle was there for the wonderings and the settling-ins. It witnessed the "this is all I have" offerings and the "please forgive us" sacrifices. It stood witness to story after story, family after family.

It was not so different from the rickety table in my mom's kitchen. Both fed families and supported heartache. Both were sacred.

God loves a good table. Chairs, on the other hand . . .

Dear Father, thank You for the tables in my life. Even if I fall off my chair, I am happy to have a place at Your table. There I am fed, loved, supported, and always part of the family. There is no place I would rather be.

LIGHT BREAD

I remember the bread dough that rose under embroidered dish towels on Grandma Gallaher's kitchen stove. I wasn't in her kitchen often, as my parents divorced when I was two, and visits to Dad's side of the family became less and less frequent. We called it "light" bread—I reckon that was because most country cooks baked biscuits and cornbread, which were much heavier. Whatever you call it, having a loaf of this sitting on your table will help your guests feel at home.

Ingredients

2 cups warm water (about 110 degrees)
$\frac{1}{4}$ cup sugar, divided
$1\frac{1}{2}$ tablespoons active dry yeast
$\frac{1}{4}$ cup vegetable oil
$1\frac{1}{2}$ teaspoons salt
4–5 cups flour
3 tablespoons melted butter

Instructions

1. In a large bowl, dissolve 1 tablespoon of sugar in warm water; then stir in yeast. Allow to sit until yeast foams—about 5 minutes.
2. Add remaining sugar and oil. Mix salt with the first cup of flour and add to bowl. Mix well. Add remaining flour 1 cup at a time, mixing with your hands or a Danish whisk until dough is tacky but pulls the flour off sides of bowl.
3. Knead dough on a floured surface for 8–10 minutes. Place in a well-oiled bowl and turn dough to coat. Cover with a damp cloth. (I use a very large Tupperware bowl and attach the lid.) Allow to rise until doubled in bulk—about an hour.
4. Divide dough into 2 equal parts. Place each loaf into a greased 9 x 5 loaf pan (or shape into circles and place on pizza stones or cookie sheets). Cover with a dish towel. Allow to rise for 30–45 minutes in a warm place, or until dough has risen 1 inch above loaf pans.
5. Bake at 350 degrees for 30–40 minutes for loaves, 15–20 minutes for rounds. Brush tops with melted butter. Recipe yields 2 standard loaves.

IF I COULDN'T CUT UP A CHICKEN

Don't pick on people, jump on their failures, criticize their faults—unless, of course, you want the same treatment.
MATTHEW 7:5, MSG

When I was a teenager, one of my uncles brought his new wife to our house so my mom could teach her how to make fried chicken. She wasn't much older than me and was less experienced in the kitchen. When Mom found out this young lady needed not only a cooking lesson but also a butchering lesson, she was appalled.

"Who in the world raises a girl without teaching her anything worthwhile? I never saw anything like it. Why, I'd be afraid to show my face in public if my daughter didn't know how to cut up a chicken."

I don't think she meant to be mean; she simply could not fathom a married woman not knowing what, to her, were the most basic of culinary skills. It truly boggled her mind.

The poor girl turned redder than a radish. I wasn't sure whether she was more embarrassed or angry. My sister stepped in and took my new aunt to wash up while I handed Mom some crackers, canned sausages, and a Pepsi.

"Well, I guess I went and did it now," Mom said as she finished her snack.

Mom isn't her best when she's feeling peckish.

She apologized, more or less, and the lesson went ahead.

By the end of the day, we had a few platters of golden fried chicken, and my aunt had gained new confidence.

Later Mom told me she needed to be nicer to my aunt. "It ain't her fault her mom didn't teach her nothin'. Bless her heart."

A few weeks later, it happened that my mom overheard someone she respected telling another person that Mom was ignorant. In my mom's mind, the only definitions for "ignorant" were "stupid," "birdbrained," and "dumb as a doornail." She had a conniption fit.

Mom truly was ignorant (unaware and uninformed) in that particular situation—but she is not stupid, birdbrained, or dumb. Mom may not know all the definitions or connotations of some words, but she knows how those words feel. She is an uneducated hillbilly, but she has country smarts to beat the band. She is the kind of woman people would run to if there were a nuclear apocalypse or zombie invasion.

It's easy to criticize. Whether we mean to or not, when we look at people solely through the lens of our experiences, we can judge harshly. People who don't know my mom could see her as just an ignorant hillbilly. That is harsh, yes, but not incorrect. However, there is so much more to her. She is loving, brave, tolerant, bold, funny, strong, protective, tenacious, loyal, welcoming, curious, and friendly. Even my chicken-frying aunt came to love Mom and spend a lot of time in our kitchen.

Judging is a funny business. The seventh chapter of Matthew talks about it quite a bit. It starts out with, "Do not judge, or you too will be judged" (7:1, NIV).

Times have changed. The majority of young women today don't know how to butcher a chicken. I'm pretty sure I know what my mom would think about that. On the other hand, when Mom was in high school, only about 50 percent of girls made it to graduation, and Mom was not one of them. Much of society would judge Mom harshly based on today's educational standards.

Jesus knows that we all have different stories. He met people from all walks of life with experiences from pampered to outcast. He loved them all. Everyone. Always. He, who could have judged them, loved them instead. I will try to leave the judging up to Him and the fried chicken up to Mom.

Dear Father, please help me to judge less. I want to be more like You—to love, to see the best in others, to expect good. Open my eyes to see people as You see them and delight in teaching, directing, and helping them.

HILLBILLY FRIED CHICKEN

Yes, in the holler, girls as young as eleven or twelve could butcher and fry chicken. Grandma Dunn fried up a couple most Sunday afternoons and served them beside potatoes, string beans, fried corn, pinto beans, cornbread, pickles, relish, deviled eggs, fried apples, and pineapple upside-down cake.

Ingredients

1 quart buttermilk

1 chicken with skin—about $2\frac{1}{2}$ pounds—cut up into 8 pieces (consult YouTube if the cutting up part is a mystery to you); or 2 pounds of precut chicken

1 teaspoon salt

1 teaspoon black pepper

1 teaspoon paprika

2 tablespoons cornstarch

1 cup all-purpose flour

2 cups vegetable, peanut, or canola oil (do not use olive oil)

$\frac{1}{4}$ cup bacon drippings (or use more oil)

Instructions

1. Pour buttermilk into a large bowl. Add chicken, cover, and let sit until chicken is no longer cold—about 20 minutes.
2. Using tongs, remove chicken from bowl and place on a wire rack.
3. In a large, sealable plastic bag, combine salt, pepper, paprika, cornstarch, and flour. Add 2 pieces of chicken to the bag and shake well to coat. Remove chicken pieces, shaking off extra flour, and return to rack. Repeat with remaining chicken.
4. Add oil and bacon drippings to a large (10- or 12-inch) cast-iron skillet or electric fryer. Heat to 350 degrees over medium heat.
5. Using tongs, add chicken pieces to oil, skin side down (avoid over-crowding the pan). The oil will drop to about 320 degrees. Cover and cook for about 6 minutes; uncover and cook an additional 9 minutes. Turn chicken pieces; cover and cook 6 minutes. Uncover and cook another 5–9 minutes, depending on the size of the pieces. If necessary, for even browning, turn pieces over a few times.
6. Drain chicken on paper towels, newspaper, or brown paper bags.
7. We drain the oil from the pan, saving a little (about 2 tablespoons) and all the crunchy pieces to make a milk gravy. Then we serve the chicken (with or without gravy) with mashed potatoes, peas, biscuits, and apple butter. Enjoy.

Women didn't "learn"
how to cook—you were
born knowing how.

EDNA LEWIS

PATIENCE AND POTATOES

I wait for the LORD, my whole being waits,
and in his word I put my hope.
PSALM 130:5, NIV

While on a trip with girlfriends to the East Coast, we stopped at a small beach café to enjoy a lobster dinner. While my friends gazed longingly at the ocean, I was laser-focused on the lobster. That experience has become one of my fondest memories. My girlfriends still talk about the look of rapture on my face as I dug into the crustacean.

A few years later, while I was on a business trip to the Philippines and Hong Kong, a native took me to an off-the-tourist-path restaurant in the Philippines and ordered for us. My plate came out with a whole fish, fried, atop a decadent sauce that made me squeal with delight.

On the same trip, a Hong Kong businessman took a group of us to a restaurant that had no English name and no English menus. I wasn't sure what appetizer we were eating, but it was—as we say in the South—finger-lickin' good. When I asked about it, the businessman told me it was duck marinated in a sauce that had been fermenting in the basement of the building since the restaurant opened fifty-some years ago.

Instant regret for asking. Some kinds of good simply need no explanation.

I have eaten a wide variety of foods from a wide variety of

cultures. But when someone asks me what food is my favorite, there's no contest—Mom's fried taters.

When I was growing up, we ate fried potatoes with almost every meal. Friends and family would show up at dinnertime hoping for some. Everyone I knew fried their potatoes, mostly in well-seasoned iron skillets like Mom's. But they didn't all taste like Mom's. Truth be told, most of them didn't hold a candle to hers.

For years I tried to understand why Mom's potatoes were so good. Was it the potatoes? We grew our own red potatoes on half an acre of prime bottomland near Grandpa's barn. But we sold them to people whose fried taters weren't nearly as good.

The skillet? Hers was antique iron and used to fry everything from squirrel to donuts. But it wasn't that unique in our neck of the woods.

The heat? We had the usual cheap electric-ring stove top that everyone else in those parts had.

The way they were cut? Most of the people I knew cut them the same way.

There was nothing special about any of it.

The one thing Mom was really good at with her potatoes— the one thing that made the difference—was neglect. She would get to puffing on her Winstons, drinking her Pepsi, talking or sewing or watching her stories (known in other parts as daytime soap operas), and plumb tune out those taters.

It was like she had a sixth sense, however, that tingled when they were about to burn. She would saunter over to the stove with a cigarette danglin' from her lips and flip the potatoes whenever the sizzle sound was just right.

I'm not sure how she knew. She just did. It was a divine gift. Her method produced a crunchy exterior and melt-in-your-mouth interior that hugged your innards all the way down.

I've watched others turn and turn and turn their potatoes when frying, creating a mushy mess that didn't have the right texture or was too greasy. It is hard not to over-turn them. The siren call of the potatoes in that hot grease calls a person to fiddle with them.

But you have to wait. Neglect. Ignore. Sit on your hands if you have to. The hope of amazing potatoes is in the waiting. And, sakes alive, is it worth it!

Just like those taters, our worries and anxieties call us to fiddle with them. We turn and turn and turn them over until our minds are mush. But our hope is in waiting on the Lord, trusting His timing. He tells us over and over in the Bible to give our troubles to Him. He knows when the time is right.

It is so hard to wait! "But if we hope for what we do not yet have, we wait for it patiently" (Romans 8:25, NIV). Not just wait. Wait *patiently*. "Be still in the presence of the LORD, and wait patiently for him to act" (Psalm 37:7).

Stop fiddling with things God is cooking. When the sizzle is right, He'll stir the pot.

Heavenly Father, thank You for having patience with me. Help me to know when to wait and when the time is right to flip things over. I need more patience to trust Your timing in every-thing—even frying potatoes.

MOM'S FRIED TATERS

Let's face it: Even bad fried potatoes are yummy. But if you can master the waiting game, you will be rewarded with potatoes that have the perfect ratio of crunch to melt-in-your-mouth goodness.

Ingredients

1½ medium (about the size of your fist) red potatoes per person
Vegetable oil, ¼ of an inch deep in skillet
Salt and pepper to taste

Instructions

1. Peel the potatoes. Rinse and pat dry.
2. Slice the potatoes into thin, french fry–sized pieces, about ⅜ of an inch thick and 1 or 2 inches long.
3. Heat oil in skillet on medium-high heat.
4. When oil is hot, pour potatoes in carefully. Liberally sprinkle salt and pepper over potatoes.
5. Let potatoes cook for about 5 minutes before flipping with a spatula. Test a small area to see whether potatoes are browning. If not, leave them alone for another couple of minutes.
6. Timing depends on heat, pan, and potato volume. Let some potatoes get golden brown on the bottom before each flip. Break up big clumps. When the centers are soft and the outsides are crispy, they are ready.

BIG BRITCHES

Saul dressed David in his own tunic. He put a coat of armor on him and a bronze helmet on his head. . . . "I cannot go in these," [David] said to Saul, "because I am not used to them." So he took them off.

1 SAMUEL 17:38-40, NIV

The first time I watched *The French Chef with Julia Child* on PBS, I was in awe. In those days, our area had two television channels on a regular basis. Two others, including PBS, came in only if the clouds were thick and the antenna had just the right amount of tinfoil wrapped around it.

That meant that watching Julia drop an ingredient or sip on her ever-present glass of wine was a rare treat. Julia showcased culinary delights like coq au vin, chocolate soufflé, and apple charlotte. I sat riveted—when I could see a whole episode.

Julia inspired me to try new things in the kitchen. Our family was big on fried turkey breast, fried potatoes, and the occasional butter pie. In high school, while staying with my dad and stepmom, I got up enough nerve to try a chocolate soufflé. I'd watched Julia bake one on TV, so surely it couldn't be that hard.

My stepmom, Lavera, aided me in my quest. When, like Julia, I got hand cramps from whisking egg whites, Lavera pulled out the electric mixer and plugged it in for me. She also helped me figure out how to make a tinfoil collar for the pan we were using so the soufflé could rise to great heights. Then we carefully slid the pan into the oven and tiptoed around the kitchen so the soufflé wouldn't fall. I had visions of a massive, fluffy delight.

The short version is that I wasn't ready for soufflé baking. There are some things you learn through error, experience, and growth. Sometimes you just have to laugh.

Our tinfoil collar fell down. The soufflé fell over. When we pulled it out of the oven, the pan appeared as if it had thrown up most of its contents. We tasted the remaining portion, only to discover cocoa lumps (a substitute for the baking chocolate Julia used) and unevenly baked batter.

Despite having to scrape baked-on chocolate from the oven racks, it was a fun adventure. Lavera still reminds me of that years-ago fiasco, and we laugh about it all over again.

I was too naive to understand the years of practice and education Julia brought to her cooking and baking. Complex French cooking fit her; it didn't fit me. I felt like a clown with huge red shoes clomping around the kitchen compared to her. Lavera said I might have been too big for my britches.

We often have a hankerin' for things we aren't really equipped for. We want to be respected, accomplished, or revered before we have done the work or learned what it takes. We want to run before we walk. Lead before we follow. Make a soufflé before we attempt homemade whipped cream. Yes, we are sometimes simply too big for our britches.

David was a teenager when he took on Goliath. He wasn't prepared. He didn't have the experience, training, or girth. Saul thought he would help the boy out by giving him the armor of a king. But David wasn't a king; he wasn't ready for that kind of equipment. He would grow into it, eventually. Until then, he stayed true to who he was and saved the day with a stone and a slingshot. If he had tried to run across that field in Saul's gear, he would have probably tripped and face-planted at Goliath's feet.

David had wisdom I did not. He knew his limits and was bold, brave, and confident in his skills and knowledge. Refusing Saul's armor, he met Goliath with the equipment that had never failed him. David had no illusions of being a mighty warrior; he simply was righting a wrong. It was the first step in a long line of steps that led to bigger britches and leading a nation.

Paul wrote to the Corinthian church, "I fed you with milk, not solid food, for you were not ready for it" (1 Corinthians 3:2, ESV). If we take things one step at a time, if we learn to walk before we run, if we sling a rock before we wield a sword, if we bake a pie before we open a bakery, we will find that God gives us the tools to grow and build the foundation we need for greater things. What we learn in those steps can be astounding.

David's confidence must have grown as much as mine deflated. He went on to rule a nation. I went back to making butter pies. And then a chocolate mousse pie, then a pavlova. And then . . . a soufflé.

Heavenly Father, when I start getting too big for my britches, humble me. Help me go step-by-step rather than jumping ahead. I trust Your recipe for my life!

BUTTER PIE

This recipe came out of the Depression era, when Grandma didn't have much more than flour, a little sugar, and lots of freshly churned butter. When the Watkins man came around selling cinnamon, hot dog! It was pie time. My mom made a lot of these.

Ingredients

1 pie crust (frozen, homemade, or refrigerated)
¾ cup sugar
6 tablespoons flour
⅔ cup milk
Pinch of salt
Ground cinnamon
¼ pound butter, cut into thin slices

Optional
1 beaten egg
2 tablespoons turbinado sugar (or sugar crystals)

Instructions

1. Preheat oven to 400 degrees. Press the pie crust into a pie plate. Turn the edges under and crimp by hand or by using a fork.
2. In a bowl, whisk the sugar, flour, milk, and salt. Pour filling into the crust. Liberally sprinkle cinnamon over the filling.
3. Dot the pieces of butter over the filling.
4. If desired, brush the exposed crust with the egg. Sprinkle sugar over the egg.
5. Bake about 25 minutes, or until the filling is set. If the edges of the crust get dark too quickly, cover the pie with aluminum foil. Let cool before slicing. Serves 8.

With enough butter,
anything is good.

JULIA CHILD

CRAVINGS

The tempter came and said to Him, "If You are the Son of God,
command that these stones become bread."

MATTHEW 4:3, NASB

We grew up drinking milk with almost every meal. That seems so foreign today, but milk is what parents used to give their children to drink with sandwiches, fried chicken, and even spaghetti. Between meals we drank water or tea, or if we timed it just right, Watkins nectar syrup mixed in fresh spring water at Grandma's.

Mom had none of this. She drank Pepsi morning, noon, and night. We were not allowed to drink her Pepsi, which was fine by me since I found it as disgusting as pig slop. My younger brother, Virgil, could connive a swig or two from her occasionally. Otherwise, the Pepsi was off-limits. It was an expense we couldn't really afford. But Mom craved it, so she took in sewing and sold Avon to pay for it.

A couple of my best friends also craved Mom's chocolate gravy and biscuits. It was on the table Saturday mornings when there was enough cocoa and sugar. We also had fried potatoes, fresh ham with streak-ed gravy (ham drippins mixed with water), and sunny-side up eggs. But when we ladled rich, dark, silky chocolate gravy over fluffy biscuits . . . I never envied biscuits so much. I guarantee that if you put that gravy on top of your head, your tongue would lick your ears off trying to get to it.

Other friends would ask to come for sleepovers on Fridays just so they could have that gravy on Saturday mornings. What I thought were friends were, in truth, fanatics who were looking for their chocolate gravy fix. I was just as hooked.

I still have a hankerin' for chocolate gravy now and then. I make it for my kids when we are together. My husband, Jeff, a Wisconsinite, hasn't developed a taste for it—yet. The weird thing is, he loves chocolate and sweets. So until he gives up the ghost, I will keep trying to convert him.

What we crave is often indicative of who we are. I long for fried potatoes and chocolate gravy. Those are the cravings of someone who grew up poor in a certain mountainous area of the country. My husband craves cookies and cherry pie. His mom packed cookies in his lunch every day of his school life. Also, in the area where he grew up, tart cherries were picked, preserved, and put in sweets by moms like his. He is a sweet northerner.

In the Bible, we're told Jesus was tempted with bread. "After fasting forty days and forty nights, he was hungry. The tempter came to him and said, 'If you are the Son of God, tell these stones to become bread'" (Matthew 4:2-3, NIV). The tempter knew how fresh bread would tempt Jesus. It was probably something Jesus dreamed about while in the desert. During Jesus' lifetime, "to eat bread" meant to have a meal. After forty days without food, the mention of bread would probably have summoned visions of a table laden with the best Hebrew foods and baskets of satisfying bread. Jesus must have been salivating!

If the tempter offered me fried potatoes or chocolate gravy after I had fasted for forty days, could I say no? He knows what to offer us. He knows, and exploits, our cravings. He waits until we are weak and vulnerable to offer us the very things we crave most.

How do we resist? We apply the same method Jesus used: "Jesus said to him, 'Away from me, Satan!'" (Matthew 4:10, NIV). We pray. We do not have the strength to say no on our own. We need divine strength.

The devil was testing Jesus, trying to trade bread for Jesus' acknowledgment that the devil's power was superior to His own. What is the devil trying to trade for your craving? Whatever it is, the trade is not worth it. Not even if he is promising never-ending chocolate gravy.

Thank You, Father, for giving us the Bread of Life. When I am tempted to satisfy a craving in exchange for anything that is not in keeping with Your Word, give me the strength to say no. Help me recognize my weaknesses and vulnerabilities so I can guard against temptation. Protect me when I am so hungry that I am willing to give up my righteousness for what the tempter is offering. You are the only Bread I need.

CHOCOLATE GRAVY

This is the way my mom made chocolate gravy. Most people would start with butter in the pan, add the dry ingredients to form a roux, then slowly add milk. But for whatever reason, Mom heated the milk first, so that is how I make it. My family also pinches off bite-sized pieces of biscuit until we have a little hill, and then we douse it in gravy.

Ingredients

4 tablespoons self-rising flour
4 tablespoons cocoa powder
1 cup sugar
½ teaspoon salt
2½ cups evaporated milk (or whole milk)
1 teaspoon vanilla
2 tablespoons butter

Instructions

1. Sift together flour, cocoa powder, sugar, and salt in a small bowl. Using a spoon, crush any remaining lumps of cocoa into the mixture.
2. In a cast-iron or heavy skillet, bring milk to a simmer over medium heat.
3. Using a whisk, slowly add dry ingredients, stirring well to avoid lumps.
4. Reduce heat to medium-low and stir until gravy thickens and bubbles. Add more milk if it seems too thick. It should be the consistency of milk gravy.
5. Remove from heat. Stir in vanilla and butter.
6. Serve over biscuits.

There is one day when all we Americans who are not self-made go back to the old home to eat saleratus biscuits and marvel how much nearer to the porch the old pump looks than it used to.

O. HENRY,
Two Thanksgiving Day Gentlemen

FLOATING PIGLETS

The rain fell and the floods came, and the winds blew
and slammed against that house; and yet it did not fall,
for it had been founded on the rock.

MATTHEW 7:25, NASB

Many improvements to our country were made during the early part of the last century when the Civilian Conservation Corps (CCC) employed jobless men to keep the economy running. My Grandpa Dunn was one of the men who worked for the CCC. He traveled all over tarnation, especially in western states, helping to construct a network of back roads, reforest woods, improve national parks, and build bridges and dams.

In our area, we saw evidence of the CCC in the perfect rows of pine trees that covered acres of national forest land and the carefully tended access roads along the mountain ridges. Most of our little gravel roads connect to the main, graded CCC roads that run along the ridge of the Ozark Mountains, high above the valleys. These roads give the folks who live in the hollers, like my family, a way to escape rising waters and forest fires.

In 1972, just after we moved out of the trailer into a new house closer to the creek, we had a doozy of a spring storm. All of the creeks and rivers started rising and kept rising. Before we knew it, little Gunnit Creek was literally at our front door. Everett, my stepdad, kept a sow with twelve babies in a pen just down the holler from our house. We could see they were about to drown as the roaring water pressed them against the wooden fencing and the babies swam for their lives. The momma was squealing like she was dying.

Everett waded through the current with a hammer and broke the fence so the pigs could float free. He wanted to keep them penned but was willing to lose pigs forever instead of letting them all drown. He tried to guide them to land, but they floated out of reach and away.

The momma made it to dry land near her pen with one baby. The rest were gone. We didn't have time to help any further, as the rain was relentless and the creek was about an inch from coming in our front door. We waded out the back, through a brisk current, and took refuge at Grandma and Grandpa's.

Everett worried over those lost pigs like a hound dog with a bone. As soon as the water started receding and it was safe, we searched the river bottoms for baby pigs. We didn't find any.

Everett drove his pickup up the holler using one of the CCC roads. High above the flooding, he made his way to the nearest feed store to find replacement food, troughs, and other things lost in the flood. While chewing the fat with the other farmers, he learned about their flooded farms, lost vehicles, and destroyed bridges. In turn, he let it be known that we had lost all those sweet little piglets. Truth be told, those piglets represented the income we would need before winter set in. We raised the pigs to sell and slaughter each fall. No pigs meant no fresh ham, bacon, or lard, and no money to have the propane tank filled.

Within days, trucks started showing up at our house. Living in the boonies as we did, it wasn't like we were easy to find—and one of the bridges had been washed out. But truck after truck showed up with a baby pig or two or three. Everett always thanked the people kindly, offered them a jar of jelly or pickles, and put the little pigs in the pen with the momma. Trucks showed up from three counties.

At the time, I couldn't understand how all these good ole boys knew how to find us. Our pigs weren't marked, and neither was our house. But they kept coming, and Everett kept smiling and accepting piglets.

We ended up with fourteen.

Sometimes on the other side of disaster are abundant blessings. Rain comes, creeks rise, pigs float away. But when we build our foundation on the Lord, the blessings find their way home.

Dear Father, when my blessings seem to be floating away, help me to trust Your foundation. You never fail me. You are my rock and my shelter. Thank You for always watching out for me when the storms come and the waters rise.

PORK TENDERLOIN WITH TART CHUTNEY

This is a recipe that will have guests asking for more. The sauce is so good I've had people ask if they could have extra to put on ice cream!

Ingredients

¾ cup cherry jam (or pear or apricot)
3 tablespoons balsamic vinegar
½ teaspoon ground cinnamon
½ teaspoon ground nutmeg
1 tablespoon olive oil
⅔ cup chopped onion
2 cups fresh or frozen tart cherries, pitted and coarsely chopped
Salt and pepper for seasoning
1¼-pound pork tenderloin

Instructions

1. Heat grill to medium.
2. While grill is heating, mix jam, vinegar, cinnamon, and nutmeg in a medium bowl. Reserve ¼ cup of mixture for glaze.
3. Add olive oil to large pan and sauté onion on stovetop over high heat for 1 minute.
4. Add cherries and jam mixture to pan. Season with salt. Simmer for approximately 8 minutes until thick, stirring often. Set aside.
5. Sprinkle pork with salt and pepper; brush with glaze.
6. On hottest part of grill, brown pork on both sides.
7. Move pork to coolest part of grill, turning and brushing with glaze often, until thermometer inserted into the thickest part of the pork reaches 145 degrees—around 25 minutes.
8. Remove pork from grill and cover with foil.
9. After 10–15 minutes, return chutney to stove and heat on medium until warmed through.
10. Slice pork and serve with warmed chutney.

BLOCKED

Their plan was to turn west into Asia province,
but the Holy Spirit blocked that route.
ACTS 16:6, MSG

Word games have been a huge thing in my family since I can remember. It started with Scrabble back when I was spelling words like *poo* and *tater*. Over time, technology and an inherited competitive nature have fueled the addiction. Now we play for bragging rights! The irritating thing is that I rule for a day, maybe two, before my sister, Carolyn, swoops in and reclaims the title.

During one particularly hard-fought battle, I had a great word ready that would use all my letters and put my score way ahead of my sister. I was waiting patiently for my chance when she blocked me. She not only played an excellent word but also blocked the only two spots that seemed to work for me.

Oh, I was spittin' fire. She was already two games up! I moved my letters around and grumbled to myself, *How could she do this to me? Now what? I can't lose to her again!*

I took a minute to refill my tea and stretch my legs. When I sat back down, I laid every tile face down and mixed them up, then turned them over one by one. I took a deep breath, looked them over, and started to see new opportunities. If I switched this and moved that and added an *s* to my sister's word, I could earn even more points than I would have before her move. She had done me a favor! I was able to play my tiles and win the game.

It reminded me how the scarcity of items we had on hand made for more interesting dishes. I would have great ideas about what to make for dinner but open the cabinets to find only half the ingredients. So I would pull them out on the table, mix them up, then line them up in a new way. A cheesy bacon cracker recipe came about when I wanted a BLT but discovered we were out of bread and tomatoes. Because I was forced to think differently, however, I invented a recipe that is lip-smacking good.

Sometimes a block is a good thing. We block babies from touching hot items to save them from burning themselves. City workers block off construction areas to keep us and our cars safe. In the same way, God blocks us when we are heading in a wrong direction.

When Paul and Timothy were traveling to Asia, the Holy Spirit blocked them not once, but twice. They ended up in the port city of Troas. I'm sure they were frustrated that their plans were not going as they had hoped. But in Troas, they were perfectly situated to cross the sea to speak to the Macedonians. God had mapped out a new route. Luke, the author of the book of Acts, wrote, "All the pieces had come together. We knew now for sure that God had called us to preach the good news to the Europeans" (Acts 16:10, MSG).

That blockage led them to Philippi, which set in motion events that led to Paul's letters to the Philippians. Their trip also saw the conversion of Lydia, who in turn changed the lives of many others. The original blockage led to events that changed history.

When God puts up blocks, it does not mean He doesn't love us. Quite the opposite. It gives us the opportunity to adjust our sails for a different, often better, destination.

Lord, help me to pay attention to the blocks that come into my life and use them to more fully follow You. When I want to quail and quit, encourage me to pray and press on. You know what is best for me. Allow me to see blocks as opportunities to try again with better results.

CHEESY BACON-WRAPPED CRACKERS

I didn't have a recipe for these back in the day, or a choice of cheese. I have since developed one that is reminiscent of those makeshift crackers that I experimented with in Mom's kitchen. They make a great appetizer for parties, football game viewing, or a night of board games.

Ingredients
12 thin bacon strips, cut in half
48 small crackers (I use Ritz)
Slices of the cheese of your choice (I use Havarti), cut into 24 1-inch squares
5–6 tablespoons brown sugar
Freshly cracked black pepper

Instructions
1. Preheat oven to 350 degrees.
2. On a baking sheet lined with parchment paper or a silicone mat, arrange the bacon strips.
3. Layer cheese between 2 crackers and place 1 cracker "sandwich" in the middle of each bacon strip.
4. Wrap the bacon around the crackers. Place on baking sheet, seam-side down.
5. Sprinkle brown sugar on top of each piece. Top with a little cracked black pepper.
6. Bake for 25–30 minutes. Cheese may ooze out a bit. (To avoid this, you can reduce heat to 250 degrees and bake for 1½ hours—if you have the patience and time.)
7. Serve at room temperature.
8. To make ahead, store cooked bacon crackers in the fridge. When ready to serve, warm in the oven at 250 degrees for about 20 minutes, or until warmed through.

Bacon is proof that God loves
us and wants us to be happy.

AUTHOR UNKNOWN

FROZEN PROCRASTINATION

The lazy man will not plow because of winter;
he will beg during harvest and have nothing.
PROVERBS 20:4, NKJV

Mom loves the outdoors. If she had her druthers, she would do all outdoor chores and no indoor ones. Gardening, stacking wood, picking witch hazel leaves to dry and sell, feeding chickens, hanging laundry—all acceptable. Anything inside usually isn't going to happen.

Her sisters and brothers regaled us over the years with stories of her indoor-chore subterfuge. She denied it, but they all agreed that her time in the outhouse after dinner outpaced her time tending to the dishes ten-to-one.

As a mother of four, Mom still preferred outdoor chores. We kids did a lot of the cooking, laundry, and dishes while she gardened, cared for the chickens, and tackled anything else that kept her outside. She would do the wash and hang the clothes on the line, but she asked us to bring them in and iron and fold them.

This was met with limited success. The apples hadn't fallen too far from the tree.

One clear winter day, she hung a load of laundry on the line in the afternoon and asked me to bring it in before I went to bed. The temperature plummeted, and I didn't want to go out there and freeze my fingers off. So I decided to wait until the sun had warmed up the world again.

The next morning, I couldn't find clean jeans when I was getting ready for school. Mom said they were on the line with the laundry I neglected to bring in. I plopped my feet into my stepdad's boots, ran through the crunchy, frosted grass out to the line, and located the jeans. They were stiff as a board. I unpinned them, and my jeans dropped from the line. Instead of falling into a heap, however, they stood upright all by themselves.

Since I needed them for school, I thought the logical next step was to warm them up in the oven. It was tough getting them crammed in there, the jeans being stiff and all. But by taking out one of the racks, I was able to force them in.

I ran to finish getting ready while they thawed. When I came back, my pants were well-done. The edges had singe marks, and the parts that were directly on the rack had grill marks lightly burned into them. I pulled my jeans out with tongs and held them outside the back door to cool for a minute. There was no time for anything else. The school bus waits for no one.

I spent the day telling anyone who would listen about the hottest new fad—singed jeans.

Procrastination coaxes us, lies to us, and makes false promises: *Doesn't it feel good right where you are? Why get up? You don't need to do that right now. There is no hurry. Tomorrow will be better, easier, faster. Just wait . . .*

I used to carry a Round Tuit in my pocket—a little coin-sized wooden disk with those exact words stamped on it. When I would think, *I'll do that when I get around to it*, that wooden Tuit would remind me not to wait—the "to it" had already been got.

The book of Proverbs warns about putting off until tomorrow what we should be doing today: "The lazy man will not plow because of winter; he will beg during harvest and have nothing" (20:4, NKJV). Like my jeans, our lives are frozen when we let procrastination take over. Instead of gaining the desired outcome, we often end up having to do more work or ruining the thing we didn't take care of in the first place.

Procrastination robs us of not only the things we want or need but also the ability to bless others. How many blessings have I missed out on because when someone asked for help, I was doing the thing I was supposed to have done yesterday? If doing the chore now opens the possible opportunity to bless others later, then why do I procrastinate? Because I do what I hate sometimes, just like Paul (Romans 7:15).

I am determined to procrastinate less and bless more. Maybe I can find another Round Tuit. I'll keep it in the pocket of my smokin' hot jeans.

Lord, thank You for revealing my procrastination. Lord, I don't want my life to be frozen in place. Give me the determination to do the things that need to be done today. Thaw out my thinking so I will be able to bless others today with the blessings You have given.

STRAWBERRY CREAM PIE

Jeans should not be frozen. This pie, however, makes frozen look good. Once you get around to making it, you won't want to put it off ever again. It is simple to make and can be frozen for a week or so. Just add the whipped cream and fruit right before serving.

Ingredients

Crust

16 chocolate sandwich cookies (like Oreos), crushed
2 tablespoons butter, melted
1 tablespoon heavy whipping cream
(Or replace with a store-bought graham cracker crust)

Pie

2 cups strawberry ice cream, softened
½ cup lemon curd
16 ounces whipped cream, divided (homemade or store bought)
2 cups fresh strawberries
½ cup fresh blueberries

Instructions

1. Preheat oven to 325 degrees. Place cookie crumbs and butter in a bowl and mix well with your hands. Add heavy whipping cream and mix again.
2. Press crust into a buttered 9-inch pie pan and chill in fridge for 10 minutes. Bake for 6 minutes. Let cool.
3. Spoon softened ice cream into cooled crust. Spread evenly. Cover with plastic wrap. Place in freezer until firm—about an hour.
4. While the ice cream hardens, fold lemon curd into half of the whipped cream. When ice cream is set, spread lemon cream over the ice cream and return to freezer for a couple of hours.
5. Wash and slice strawberries. Rinse and dry blueberries.
6. Remove pie from freezer and top with remaining whipped cream and fruit. Serves 8.

LOVE IS A VERB

Love bears all things, believes all things,
hopes all things, endures all things.
1 CORINTHIANS 13:7, esv

My stepfather loved liver and onions. Every time Mom cooked up a skillet, the smell would entice me into the kitchen. I would stealthily sidle over to the stove, lift the lid from the pan, and groan in utter disappointment. How could something smell so good and taste so nasty?

There was no escaping it. That sautéed onion smell permeated every surface in the house and made my mouth water, but the taste of the liver was sharp, earthy, and metal-lic. We ate a lot of wildlife, but liver is gamey on a whole other level.

Mom wasn't the kind of parent who made her kids eat everything on the table. But she did ask us to try everything. That liver made me gag. I disliked it so much, my brother Mike would put a piece on his fork and chase me around the table just to aggravate me.

At least Mom served the liver with mashed potatoes and veggies.

The other big disappointing smell came the few times Mom tried to make pinto beans. Pintos need to cook for hours. Mom would put a pot of them on to boil, go outside to work in the garden, and ultimately forget all about the beans.

116

Have you ever smelled burned beans? They stink high to heaven. We had to put the charred pot outside, open the windows, and turn on fans. The scent was everywhere—in the carpet, the drapes, the pillows, our hair. It lingered for days. It was hard to eat other food with that odor commandeering our senses.

Both smells were evidence of love. Mom hates beans, but she cooked them because she loved my stepdad. She knew he loved them, so she tried. Thankfully Grandma and her perfect beans were right down the road.

Mom's way of loving people was by doing. She fed people. She welcomed, she shared, she opened her home to the down-and-out. She gave rides to people who didn't have cars. She sewed, cooked, crafted, defended, volunteered, and chaired. Mom wasn't big on sentimentality—she was big on practicality. She loved with action.

When I peel a tangerine, I am instantly transported to Mom's kitchen. We had fruit only when nature provided it: blackberries we picked ourselves, peaches from Grandma Dunn's tree, watermelons from the patch in the dog days of summer. Fruit that we couldn't grow ourselves wasn't on Mom's table. We simply couldn't afford it—except at Christmas. Then, and only then, Mom bought fancy nuts and tangerines. And those tangerines . . . Lord, have mercy! They were more anticipated than Santa. Every piece of peel removed revealed another slice of sunshine—and the aroma would take you over. They perfumed the whole season.

As an adult, I wonder what Mom gave up for us to have those tangerines. They didn't come with our commodities—she needed cash to buy them. That meant something had to be sacrificed. Whatever it was, she gave it up without a word so tangerine juice could drip off our elbows. What a gift.

We are conditioned by the world to think that love is a feeling we have no control over—as though love were mysterious and sometimes devious. But is it? Paul wrote that love "does not insist on its own way" (1 Corinthians 13:5, ESV). Love is a verb, an action, a choice. "Let us not love with words or speech but with actions and in truth" (1 John 3:18, NIV).

Love buys tangerines, cooks liver, and accidentally burns beans.

Love never disappoints.

What does disappoint? Liver. Liver disappoints.

Jesus, thank You for choosing to love me. Thank You for blessings like tangerines and people who love by doing. Jesus, help me to be love in action.

EASY TANGERINE JAM

This jam is easy, fresh, and bright. It takes morning toast to new heights. But it is also scrumptious between layers of a coconut or pineapple cake.

Ingredients

3 pounds tangerines, peeled and cut in half,
  seeds removed
1 cup sugar
Juice of 2 lemons, seeds removed

Instructions

1. Process the tangerines in a food processor until smooth, working in batches if necessary.
2. Pour into a large, heavy pot; then add the sugar and lemon juice.
3. Bring the mixture to a boil, reduce heat, and gently boil for about 30 minutes, stirring often. Do not cover.
4. The mixture will thicken and turn more glossy when it is ready. Test by dropping jam onto a frozen plate. If the jam firms up, it's done. If not, boil a little longer.
5. When set, ladle jam into clean jars, cover the tops loosely, and let cool on the counter.
6. When the jars reach room temperature, tighten jar lids and refrigerate. Jam will keep a week or two in the fridge. Makes 3 cups.

Memory believes before
knowing remembers.

WILLIAM FAULKNER,
Light in August

HELP

*Martha was distracted with all her preparations; and she came
up to Him and said, "Lord, do You not care that my sister has
left me to do the serving by myself? Then tell her to help me."*
LUKE 10:40, NASB

My sister, bless her heart, was Martha to my Mary. Carolyn
was obedient, disciplined, and quiet, and she seemed to
know how to pick up, clean up, and put things away as a matter
of course. I was strong-willed, undisciplined, loud—and could
step over a million things without seeing them. I still can.

About once a month, Mom would buy us these amazing
frozen glazed donuts. Since the nearest bakery was an hour
away, the frozen kind were as close as we got to fresh yeast
donuts. Carolyn would pop a few in the oven before school, and
we would have hot, sticky donuts by the time we had gotten
ourselves dressed and ready.

Until she didn't.

"Where are the donuts?" I asked one morning.

"If you want some, fix them yourself," she answered. "I am
not your slave."

Then she just walked away, leaving me there to starve.

I was the kid who would stand in front of the kitchen sink
for hours determined not to do the dishes until I was good and
ready to do them. Muleheaded, some may call it. Decisive is a
nicer term. So, true to form, I refused to bake the donuts.

She didn't care. She was eating rabbit food at that time in her life. My brothers Mike and Virgil sure weren't baking the donuts. I was the only one missing them.

I cut off my nose to spite my face on that one. I made chocolate toast instead.

In this way, I was very much like Mom. As girls, we both tried to get out of work drudgery because we wanted to be where the fun was. But because of that, we missed so much. Think of all the time I could have had with family and friends if I had just done the dishes when asked. While I was standing in front of the sink, they were playing cards, talking, and enjoying life.

When Martha was complaining about Mary (Luke 10:40), she just wanted help. She, like Carolyn, was probably tired of dealing with a sister she perceived as muleheaded and lazy. She focused on the work and expected Mary to focus on the same things.

When Mary didn't, Martha probably threw herself more and more into her work and bitterness. The work became more important than the reason she was doing the work: to celebrate Jesus. Martha wasn't celebrating, but Mary was—so much so that she left her sister high and dry again. For a good reason, but alone in the kitchen just the same.

I have been both Mary and Martha. I know what it is to be the one needing help and the one not helping. I've learned that when I need help, I have to ask for it. When I don't, I start imagining all kinds of reasons why the person isn't lending a hand. I run around like a chicken with its head cut off and am offended by anyone who isn't doing the same.

Yet when I'm the one not giving assistance, I rarely realize it is needed. I am so focused that I'm oblivious to others slaving away.

When we focus on the helping or the avoidance of helping, we miss the point. Jesus is our focal point. Jesus first, then others. Jesus tells us in the Gospel of Mark, "Love the Lord your God with all your heart, all your soul, all your mind, and all your strength." Then He says, "Love your neighbor as yourself" (12:30-31). Love is all you need.

Love and glazed donuts.

Lord, forgive me for being stubborn! Thank You for both Marthas and Marys. Help me to be the best of both. When I am so caught up in being decisive that all I think about is me, refocus my attention on You. I love You, Lord!

CHOCOLATE TOAST

For a simple, quick breakfast, nothing beats chocolate toast. It's not the same as a glazed donut, but it will satisfy your sweet tooth in minutes.

Ingredients

2 teaspoons cocoa
4 tablespoons sugar
4 slices of good bread
2 tablespoons softened (not melted) butter

Instructions

1. Position oven rack 4 inches from the broiler element and preheat oven to 400 degrees.
2. Mix cocoa and sugar together in a small bowl.
3. Liberally spread butter over one side of each bread slice. Place bread, butter side up, on baking sheet.
4. Sprinkle cocoa mixture over butter.
5. Bake for 3–4 minutes, until sugar bubbles. If sugar is not melting, turn on broiler for a minute. Watch closely so it doesn't burn.
6. Bottom should be lightly toasted. Serves 2.

PEEL AND PRAY

Keep on asking, and you will receive what you ask for.
Keep on seeking, and you will find. Keep on knocking,
and the door will be opened to you.

LUKE 11:9

My family's love of potatoes exceeds sanity. We had them with every meal—fried, mashed, baked, sautéed, casseroled, hashed, roasted, french fried, souped, and stewed. They showed up in donuts and on pizza. Potatoes are nothing if not versatile.

Hours of my childhood were dedicated to peeling potatoes. I was waist-high to a grasshopper when I started peeling them. Our family didn't believe in vegetable peelers. What nonsense. A pocketknife or a big ole carving knife could get the job done in seconds. It was nothing to peel a bag of potatoes during a commercial break and be back in time to catch the end of our favorite show.

One Thanksgiving I peeled pounds of potatoes. The city cousins were down, which meant we had been up half the night playing spoons or Monopoly or rummy. Not wanting to miss a thing, I crept out of bed the next morning at the first sound of stirring in the kitchen, stepping over a few people on pallets to join Mom and a couple of aunts who were drinking coffee and preparing the food to come. I was handed a knife and a bin of potatoes. I peeled and peeled, and at some point I fell asleep at the table with potatoes pillowing my head and the knife in my hand. Mom gently removed the knife, woke me, and set me to peeling again.

I peeled all those potatoes. I still peel potatoes. And I will peel more in the future.

I peeled, I peel, I will peel.

In that same kitchen, on that same table, I have also fallen asleep praying. There were prayers that needed to be prayed. I prayed them, nodded off, woke up, and kept praying. I did not pray once and stop. I continued to pray.

Both the Gospels of Matthew (chapter 6) and Luke (chapter 11) include the Lord's Prayer. When Jesus was teaching His disciples this prayer, they were already praying men who had been praying since they could talk. He gave them a new prayer radically different from the ceremonial prayers they were used to.

Then He followed that up with more teaching on prayer: "I tell you, keep on asking, and you will receive what you ask for. Keep on seeking, and you will find. Keep on knocking, and the door will be opened to you. For everyone who asks, receives. Everyone who seeks, finds. And to everyone who knocks, the door will be opened" (Luke 11:9-10).

It is not enough to pray it and forget it. Jesus says to keep praying. If you feel your prayer hasn't been answered, keep praying. If it has been answered, keep praying. You may find that there is more to the answer or the blessing than you originally thought. And there is always room for more thanksgiving.

The biggest advantage of continual prayer, however, is closeness to God—talking, listening, communing with Him.

I prayed, I pray, I will pray. And then I will peel more potatoes.

Thank You, Jesus, for teaching me to pray. I want to be close to You, so help me to pray and keep praying. Hear me and open my ears so I hear You. No matter what happened yesterday, what is happening today, or what happens tomorrow, help me to pray through it all.

GRILLED ONIONS AND POTATOES

This simple side dish is something I make when we are low on grocer-
ies. Potatoes and onions are always in the bin, and there's usually
a can of beans in the cupboard. It makes an excellent side dish for
grilled meats and can be cooked on the same charcoal or gas grill.

Ingredients

1 can (15.5 ounces) cannellini (or white, pinto, or black) beans,
  drained
2 large russet potatoes, sliced $\frac{1}{4}$ of an inch thick
1 medium red onion, peeled and sliced
3 tablespoons olive oil, divided
1 teaspoon Dijon mustard
1 lemon, juiced and seeds removed
1 teaspoon chopped fresh rosemary
$\frac{1}{2}$ teaspoon crushed red pepper flakes
Salt and pepper

Instructions

1. Drain beans and set aside.
2. Heat grill pan or stove-top grill to medium-high heat.
3. Toss potato and onion slices with 1 tablespoon oil in medium bowl.
4. Place potato and onion slices on grill pan. Do not overlap. Cook
   in batches as needed. Cook 3–4 minutes on each side, until lightly
   browned and potato is cooked in the middle.
5. Return to bowl. Add beans.
6. Mix mustard, remaining olive oil, and lemon juice in a small bowl.
   Pour over potatoes.
7. Sprinkle vegetables with rosemary and red pepper flakes and season with salt and pepper to taste.
8. Serve warm. Serves 2.

There is all the pleasure that
one can have in gold-digging in
finding one's hopes satisfied in the
riches of a good hill of potatoes.

SARAH ORNE JEWETT,
The Country of the Pointed Firs

BLESSED TO BLESS

Give, and you will receive. Your gift will return to you in full—pressed down, shaken together to make room for more, running over, and poured into your lap. The amount you give will determine the amount you get back.

LUKE 6:38

In the sixties and seventies, hordes of people left their nine-to-five city lives for communal country living. They hand-built homes and lived off the land. Many practiced holistic medicine, grew their own crops, and enjoyed a peaceful, quiet life.

Our little holler had one of these communities. About a mile up the road from our house lived a few doctors, lawyers, restaurateurs, professors, and other professionals in what we called Hippie Holler. Some brought their families, and some left them behind.

There was a lot of gossip about the folks up in Hippie Holler. Basically, the run-of-the-mill country folk were plumb ignorant about hippies and didn't understand what those city folk were running away from. Their gossip was innocent curiosity. The not so run-of-the-mill folk? Well, all I can say is, some people are meaner than a striped snake. They just made things up about them.

Mom, on the other hand, couldn't wait to get to know them. As soon as it was neighborly, we loaded some canned goods and cornbread in a basket, piled into the pickup, and headed up the holler. I stood in the back, leaning against the cab as we bounced up a road that became more and more like a ditch.

When their clearing came in sight, I was gobsmacked. There were four or five tepees, each covered in white cloth. Some had smoke puffing out of the holes in the tops. In another area, men were constructing a long house out of hand-skinned logs. But what flabbergasted me most was the women planting seeds in a big garden patch. It looked like they were nekked on top. Heavens to Betsy! I slapped my hands over my eye sockets faster than a ghost can say boo.

Slowly I peeked between my fingers and saw that the women were actually wearing halters or bras dyed about the same color as their skin. Those old gossips had me believing we would find women doing nude organic gardening up there. They lied. What else were they wrong about?

Turns out those hippies were nice as could be. They appreciated being welcomed to the neighborhood. Mom loaded them up with food, offered the use of our phone, and promised to come back to check on them directly.

At first, they accepted all the food we could spare. But soon enough their garden produced pretty near all they needed. They finished their house and became self-sufficient, other than borrowing our phone from time to time over the years and hitching a ride when they needed it. Mom and Everett invited them to our summer barbecues and camping adventures, and they became lifelong friends.

We may not have been eating filet mignon, but we always had enough food to share. We were blessed with bottomland that nurtured immense gardens, creeks that provided fish, forests that sheltered abundant wildlife, family who loved and supported us, and country smarts enough to show a few city slickers a trick or two. We were blessed.

And we shared our blessings. When we had cheese, we shared cheese. When we had cornbread, we shared cornbread. Jesus said, "Give, and you will receive. Your gift will return to you in full—pressed down, shaken together to make room for more, running over, and poured into your lap" (Luke 6:38).

The friends we made from Hippie Holler helped Mom and Everett many times over the years. One of the lawyers, who eventually became our county's prosecuting attorney, represented them in legal matters. Others helped us dig out after the big flood that destroyed the pigpens and chicken coops. They ended up helping us as much as or more than we ever helped them. We blessed and were blessed in turn.

When we recently laid Everett to rest, friends from Hippie Holler were there among the mourners. Their presence added a layer of blessing to a hard but sweet celebration of life. Our gifts were returned in full, running over, and standing there beside us.

Lord, thank You for blessing me with friends and family. Help me to use the blessings You give me to bless others. May I see even the tiniest blessing as a gift that can be shared. And Lord, help me to never believe gossip. Instead, open my heart to friendships and connections with people who are different from me.

WATERCRESS AND MUSHROOM OMELET

Aunt Jean and Mom helped the hippies forage for wild watercress. It was plentiful in the area, especially downstream from the low-water bridges. Watercress is considered a superfood, although we didn't know that at the time. Use whatever mushrooms are in season. Morels, which are in season about the same time as spring watercress, make an excellent choice.

Ingredients

½ cup morel or other mushrooms, sliced
2 teaspoons olive oil
Salt and pepper to taste
¼ cup packed watercress (or kale or chard)
3 eggs
2 teaspoons half-and-half
1 tablespoon unsalted butter
3 tablespoons grated cheese (Parmesan, aged Gouda, Cheddar, Swiss, or whatever is on hand)
Green onion, both white and green parts sliced thin

Instructions

1. Sauté mushrooms in olive oil over medium heat for about 8 minutes. Sprinkle with salt and pepper; set aside.
2. Roughly chop watercress, then stir into hot mushrooms. The heat should wilt the watercress.
3. Whisk eggs and half-and-half. Season with salt and pepper.
4. Melt butter in an omelet pan, or the sauté pan you used earlier, over medium-high heat; swirl to coat pan. Carefully pour eggs into center of skillet. Reduce heat to medium.
5. As eggs set, move them toward center of pan; then tip skillet to allow uncooked eggs to fill in outer edges until set.
6. Top half of eggs (one side of omelet) with sautéed mushrooms and watercress, along with 2 tablespoons cheese. Remove from burner. Carefully use a spatula to fold other half of omelet over mushrooms, watercress, and cheese.
7. Let set in pan about 30 seconds; then gently slide omelet onto a plate.
8. Sprinkle the final tablespoon of cheese and green onion slices over top of omelet. It should be enough to share with a friend!

A FRESH PERSPECTIVE

Wise men and women are always learning,
always listening for fresh insights.
PROVERBS 18:15, MSG

For most of my life, I was a jock. My circle of friends was almost completely made up of volleyball players and other athletes. In high school, most of my teammates were related to me, one way or another. College volleyball, however, opened up a whole new world. I met girls from all over the country. Yes, I met other hillbillies, but I met girls from backgrounds that were foreign and exciting.

One of them once invited me and several girls to spend a weekend at her home. I couldn't wait to go. Vicky lived in a small town not much bigger than the one I was bussed to for school, but her father had been in the military and traveled the globe. She seemed sophisticated and cultured compared to the rest of us. The idea that she had been exposed to a life outside of our area was fascinating.

Vicky's father had done his military service in Okinawa, Japan, where he met and married his wife. She was lovely. Her English was a bit stilted, but her heart was warm and welcoming. And her kitchen smelled like nothing I had ever encountered. I had a million questions. She probably thought I was a nuisance.

At one point during the weekend, the rest of the girls went

outside to shoot hoops. I stayed inside to nose around the kitchen. When I saw Vicky's mom making what looked like filled dumplins, I had to find out what she was creating. By repeating ourselves a few times and using hand gestures, the two of us—a nosy hillbilly and a beautiful Asian mom—were able to communicate very well. She shared her recipe for gyozas with me. And I fell in love!

Gyozas were something I had never met before; they are similar to Chinese pot stickers. I honestly don't remember anything else that was served for dinner that evening. My love affair with gyozas was immediate and consuming—I only had eyes for them.

I was surrounded by great friends, laughter, and good food during that visit. It was amazing to try new and different things. Until then, Rice-A-Roni was about as adventurous as I got. The hospitality extended to me by a woman who lived in a small Missouri town, thousands of miles from her home in Japan, showed me the true reach of sharing a meal.

Over the years, her recipe has become one of my most requested. Even people who don't traditionally like pot stickers love Vicky's mom's gyozas. The experience was the beginning of a culinary curiosity that has taken my palate to new heights. I watched, listened, and received insight into a wider world of food. It literally changed me.

One step off the beaten path led to a whole new perspective. The same happens in our spiritual lives. When we open our minds to listen to the urging of the Holy Spirit, even when we don't understand all that's being communicated, and take the time to look into what the Bible says, we gain insight and wisdom. "Wise men and women are always learning, always listening for fresh insights," as Proverbs 18:15 tells us (MSG). In doing so, we develop a stronger faith, a more focused vision, and a broader understanding of the spiritual world around us.

Later that year, Vicky lost her parents in a car accident. I sometimes think about those few hours I had with them and grieve the visits, recipes, and memories that were not to be. I'm extremely thankful for that little slice of time in her mom's kitchen and the recipe that is one of my all-time favorites. But more than that, I am thankful for a caring, loving family that welcomed me with open arms and changed my culinary perspective forever.

Lord, surprise me! Introduce me to new people, places, and recipes. Open my eyes and ears to new insights. Thank You for every person who has and will enlighten my outlook on Your creative world.

VICKY'S MOM'S GYOZAS

Although this is not your typical down-South or homegrown recipe,
it is a nice change from heavier fried foods found on many Southern
tables. Most of the ingredients are inexpensive and easy to find. Most
grocery stores carry the wrappers in the fresh produce section.

Ingredients

Gyozas
½ pound raw ground beef, turkey, or chicken
½ pound raw ground pork
1 large carrot, grated
3 green onions, chopped fine
4 tablespoons soy sauce
1 package (80) wonton wrappers

Dipping Sauce
Juice from 1 fresh lemon (about 3 tablespoons)
3 tablespoons soy sauce
½ green onion, chopped fine
1 teaspoon toasted sesame seeds
1 tablespoon sweet chili sauce (optional)

Instructions

1. Mix meat, carrot, onion, and soy sauce together in a bowl until
   mixed through. Do not overmix.
2. Put 1 spoonful of meat mixture in the middle of each wrapper.
3. Wet edges of wrapper and fold in half diagonally. Place on a
   cookie sheet and keep covered with a damp paper towel. Repeat process until all meat is used.
4. Heat a cast-iron or nonstick skillet on medium heat.
5. When pan is hot, lay 6–8 gyozas in the pan. Don't overcrowd. Cook on
   one side for about a minute, until they have a golden-brown crust.
6. Turn and brown the other side of each gyoza for about a minute.
7. When that side is browned, add 1 tablespoon water and immediately
   put a lid on the pan. Let it steam until all the water is evaporated.
   The gyozas should release from the pan when they are fully cooked.
8. For the dipping sauce, mix ingredients (include optional chili sauce
   if desired) in a small bowl. Serve sauce on the side with gyozas.

One place understood helps us
understand all places better.

EUDORA WELTY,
One Writer's Beginnings

Part 3

COME SIT A SPELL WITH ME

I can with one eye squinted
take it all as a blessing.

FLANNERY O'CONNOR,
The Habit of Being

DOG HAIR AND LOCUSTS

John's clothes were woven from coarse camel hair,
and he wore a leather belt around his waist.
MATTHEW 3:4

I met an extraordinary lady when we were preparing for a short missions trip. Darla and I hit it off at the first preparation meeting. As we got to know each other before, during, and after that trip, we discovered how much we had in common. We both are old-fashioned at heart. We both grew up on working farms. We both do a lot of crafting, make things from scratch, and love repurposing whatever we can. Darla spins her own yarn on a spinning wheel that is older than she is. And she pieces together amazing stained glass windows.

Her husband, Terry, died from an inherited disease several years before I met her. She knew when she married him that, at best, they would have twenty years together. They had less than that, but they enjoyed lots of adventures before he passed away. Their family included one rambunctious biological son, Shawn, and two adopted handicapped children, Molly and Christopher.

Darla told me stories of pushing Terry's wheelchair while pulling her adopted son's wheelchair, keeping an eye on Molly's jerky progress, and hoping Shawn—who was more like Curious George than a small boy—would stay harnessed to one of the chairs. They trudged up mountains, walked through parks, and made it to church Sunday after Sunday.

By the time I met Darla, Shawn was an adult. Due to complications from their individual diseases, Terry and Christopher had died on the same date one year apart, and Molly had moved away. Darla and Shawn were a close, crafty, animal-loving family. At that time, Shawn had a dog, Laddie, who was failing in health. Every time I was at their house, Darla was combing Laddie. I thought it interesting that she saved the hair in a big bag. With each visit, the bag was notice-ably fuller.

After Laddie passed away, Darla took all that hair and spun it into yarn. I didn't even know you could do that! And I won-dered why someone would want to. I mean, what if it got wet—would it have that wet-dog smell? I thought she had completely flipped her lid.

But she had a plan. She spun the dog hair together with beautiful wool on that old spinning wheel, then dyed the result-ing yarn with homemade vegetable dye. It was perfect for the charming winter sweater she knitted for Shawn.

Who would have thought? What seemed like a bad ward-robe choice was actually a sentimental remembrance. Shawn wore that sweater with pride. (I may have spilled water on his sleeve just to see whether it would have that wet-dog smell. Surprisingly, it smelled like a sweater.)

When I was reading the Bible through a giggly teenage-girl lens, I remember thinking how gross John the Baptist must have been. He ate locusts and wore a camel hair coat. I won-dered why those details were included in the story of Jesus. Have you met a locust? They eat every plant in their path—even the yucky ones. Why would anyone eat them?

As an adult, I realized one reason these details were included was to identify John as the "one crying in the wilderness," whom Isaiah prophesied about (Isaiah 40:3, NKJV). That revelation would have been important to the Jewish people of Jesus' time. Those paying attention would know their Messiah was on the way.

But perhaps another reason was to give a fuller understanding of who John was. He was humble, his ministry was more important than his wardrobe, and he lived off the land. He not only believed his mission was to pave the way for the Messiah but also preached it, lived it, magnified it every single day.

John's lifestyle said a lot about his heart—just like Shawn's did. By wearing the sweater his mom had made him, Shawn showed respect for his mom, his sentimentality, and his unique personality. He and Darla helped me see John the Baptist in a new light.

John wasn't gross at all. He was an amazing, one-of-a-kind prophet who helped set a new world in motion while wearing a camel hair sweater.

Dear God, thank You for the unusual, unique, and one-of-a-kind people in my life. Help me to always see people for who they are, not how they appear. Thank You for helping my view of the Bible continue to develop.

SAUSAGE AND SAUERKRAUT

One of the ingredients Darla and I enjoy that many others find old-fashioned is sauerkraut. This recipe is similar to the one my mom frequently made. A friend from Germany influenced the recipe, so it has developed into a more modern and tasty version.

Ingredients

2 pounds sauerkraut, rinsed and drained (we used 2 pint jars)
$\frac{1}{4}$ cup brown sugar
1 apple, diced
$\frac{1}{2}$ pound bacon, diced
1 large onion, chopped
1$\frac{1}{2}$ pounds smoked sausage or kielbasa, cut into 1-inch slices

Instructions

1. In a large saucepan, mix the sauerkraut, brown sugar, and apple. Using medium-low heat, bring mixture to a simmer. Turn to low heat and cook for 1$\frac{1}{2}$–2 hours, stirring occasionally.
2. Heat a medium skillet over medium heat. Once hot, cook the bacon and onion until the bacon is almost crisp and the onion is beginning to brown, 10–12 minutes. Add the bacon mixture into the sauerkraut mixture, leaving some bacon grease in the pan for the sausage.
3. Fry the sausage in the remaining bacon grease until it is brown on all sides, 10–15 minutes. Add sausage to sauerkraut and stir. Simmer for another 20 minutes or so.
4. Serve with a big slice of homemade bread (see Light Bread recipe on page 79) topped with butter or apple butter.

YES. NO. YES. NO!

*I do not understand what I do. For what I want to do
I do not do, but what I hate I do.*

ROMANS 7:15, NIV

There is nothing more exasperating than slaving over an amazing dinner or pouring your heart into a dessert, only to hear your guest say, "Oh, I'm dieting. Do you have a carrot? Celery, perhaps?"

I get it. We are a dieting nation. In 2019 the dieting industry was valued at $72 billion. *Billion!* Can you believe it? People love to diet; or they love to eat and want to feel better about it, so they start a diet program. But don't start one before coming to my house. We have no celery here.

Grandma Dunn's first question whenever I walked into her house was, "Do you want something to eat?" She would warm up beans and cornbread or put a piece of fried chicken between biscuit layers or, at the very least, pour a glass of milk and pull out the sugar wafers. Remember those wafers? The ones Grandma kept had vanilla, chocolate, and strawberry in one package. Her stash never failed her. Every time she opened the cabinet they were there—self-replenishing cookies! She let me believe the baking elves lived in there.

Maybe that has been my problem: I believe food should be plentiful and never-ending—a thought process that has led me to become one of the millions of dieters. I am off diets more than I am on them, but over the years I have tried keto, the Abs Diet, Atkins, Weight Watchers, and the nasty lemon/maple syrup/cayenne pepper one. That one really got my goat. Now I even struggle to put maple syrup on pancakes.

When it comes down to it, we all know what will keep us healthy: good choices. Every bite is a choice. Moving instead of sitting is a choice. Praying instead of stressing is a choice. It is not always easy, but unless we have a prohibitive medical condition, our health is up to us. If we really want to change, we can.

When baking elves live in the cabinets and call to you when you are hungry, however, it is hard to choose the right thing over the easy or tasty thing. That's when I feel like the apostle Paul: I know what I want to do, but I do what I hate. Temptation is around every corner and hiding in every cabinet. I say no, no, no. The temptation says yes, yes, yes. *Yes. No. Yes. No!*

"The trouble is with me, for I am all too human" (Romans 7:14).

The problem is, temptation uses the things that we see as good, pleasurable, or satisfying to trip us up. If a little is good, it says, then more is better. Two donuts are better than one. Another glass of wine won't hurt. The bed is so comfy; I'll work (or work out) later. It isn't that we exactly say yes to temptation. We simply slide into it before we think to say no.

Our desire is to be people who have it under control. We fight to put our yeses and noes in the right order—to embrace the celery. And we fail.

"Thank God! The answer is in Jesus Christ our Lord" (Romans 7:25). He never fails. His yeses and noes are right where they are supposed to be. Go to Him in prayer when you are tempted. He listens. His words in the Bible—which are now available through an app on your always-with-you phone—direct, encourage, enlighten, soothe, and strengthen. With His help, temptation is much easier to handle.

And who knows—maybe He will also help us like celery.

Dear Father, thank You for giving me the strength to say no to the things that could trip me up. Show me the right path when temptations sneak into my life, and give me the determination to always walk with You.

CELERY SALAD

This is the salad for when your dieting friends ask whether you have any celery! Paired with sweet cranberries and sour lemon juice, it ramps up diet food.

Ingredients

½ cup raw almonds

8 celery stalks, thinly sliced on a diagonal, leaves separated and
    coarsely chopped

½ cup dried cranberries or raisins

Kosher salt and freshly ground black pepper

3 tablespoons fresh lemon juice

⅔ cup Parmesan, shaved (about 2 ounces)

¼ cup extra-virgin olive oil

Instructions

1. Preheat oven to 350 degrees. Spread almonds on a small, rimmed baking sheet; toast, stirring occasionally, until golden brown—about 8 minutes. Let cool; coarsely chop.
2. Toss almonds, celery, celery leaves, and cranberries in a medium bowl; season with salt and pepper.
3. Mix lemon juice, Parmesan, and oil. Pour over salad and toss gently. Serves 6.

CHOCOLATE-COVERED CONCLUSIONS

Naaman went away angry and said, "I thought
that he would surely come out to me and stand and call
on the name of the LORD his God, wave his hand over
the spot and cure me of my leprosy."

2 KINGS 5:11, NIV

"**D**id you eat Daddy's cake?"

"Um . . . no. It not me," said the miniature human,
smeared from head to toe in chocolate as she licked the excess
off her fingers.

I turned to look in the kitchen. The fridge was standing
open. Chocolate was all over its handle, the floor, and a few
cabinets. Goodness gracious, it was everywhere.

When I looked back at Jasmine, she was licking icing
from her shirt! I yelled a bit, picked up the little human,
unceremoniously deposited her into the shower, and washed
her—clothes and all.

I was madder than a wet hen. I had left the little cyclone
alone for only five minutes. I never should have let her help make
the cake to begin with. She had watched me put it in the fridge
after it was finished. Now it was probably ruined. Or was it?

"Sweetie, where did you get the chocolate?" I asked as I
was toweling her off.

"From the friggerstraighter."

"Did you get it from Daddy's cake?"

"No, from the tubberswears."

When I took the time to actually look in the fridge, the cake was undisturbed. The "tubberswears" holding the leftover icing was upside down on the shelf and emptier than Scrooge's heart. She hadn't destroyed the cake, just the kitchen.

Even though I felt like having a hissy fit, I sat on the floor, took a deep breath, and said a quick prayer for patience. Jasmine came into the room brushing her wet hair out of her face. She climbed into my lap and said, "I sorry, Momma."

How could I be angry with the cute little munchkin after that? She hadn't ruined the cake; she had only celebrated her love of chocolate. We cleaned up the mess and had a great birthday dinner when her daddy got home.

I'm a Christian, but I yell a little. I had jumped to a conclusion and yelled out of anger—over a little smeared chocolate.

If jumping to conclusions were a sport, I am sure I could be an Olympian. Part of that comes from those years when I needed to put two and two together before one of my children burned down the house.

Another part comes from being wise in my own eyes, as Proverbs 3:7 says. I often think I know what is going on when I really don't.

Some of it is a genuine character flaw. One of Solomon's Proverbs reminds us to use restraint: "Don't jump to conclusions—there may be a perfectly good explanation for what you just saw" (Proverbs 25:8, MSG). In other words, don't think you know everything.

In the book of 2 Kings, Naaman, a great army commander suffering from leprosy, jumped to conclusions. His king sent him to Israel for healing. The king couldn't heal him, so the great prophet Elisha stepped in. Elisha sent a message to the warrior that described a simple method for ridding him of his leprosy: "Go and wash yourself seven times in the Jordan River" (2 Kings 5:10).

What in tarnation? Naaman was peeved. He thought the Israelites were playing him. He was nearabout to storm off into the desert when one of his officers talked some sense into him: *Just try it. Don't assume that the simplicity of the action negates the power of the miracle.*

Of course, Naaman dipped in the Jordan seven times and was cured.

Not, however, before he huffed off in a rage because he had jumped to a conclusion. Just imagine the life Naaman could have missed out on if he hadn't backed that truck up and done the thing he didn't understand.

Drawing wrong conclusions happens when little girls smear chocolate on kitchen floors and when warriors think answers are too simple. We see. We assess. We assume.

Thankfully Jesus doesn't. He watches. He understands. He knows.

Thank You, God, for knowing me. When I do things that make the world jump to conclusions, You know my heart and have my back. Thank You. Help me look into hearts and not jump to conclusions when I'm dealing with others. I want to be more like You.

AUNT JOAN'S CHOCOLATE ICING

This is the best chocolate icing for donuts. It can also be poured over cake or cupcakes or spread over biscuits for a sweet treat. It is supersimple but massively satisfying. It is also sticky and gooey and wonderful. You may find yourself licking it off your shirt.

Ingredients

1 cup sugar
2 heaping tablespoons cocoa
1 12-ounce can of evaporated milk
1 tablespoon butter
2 teaspoons vanilla

Instructions

1. Mix sugar, cocoa, and evaporated milk in a medium saucepan.
2. Bring to a boil, stirring frequently until mixture thickens.
3. Stir in butter and vanilla until melted. Remove from heat.
4. Dip donuts into hot icing and cool on waxed paper.

FINGERPRINTS

When I consider your heavens, the work of your fingers,
the moon and the stars, which you have set in place,
what is mankind that you are mindful of them,
human beings that you care for them?
PSALM 8:3-4, NIV

I have a . . . let's call her an acquaintance . . . who is very meticulous about food preparation and disposal. Every grain of food left in a pot or on a plate must be removed with a rubber spatula, the spatula scraped clean with a butter knife, and the knife scraped (or sometimes licked) within a quarter inch of its nickel core. Those scrapings are put in a paper towel that is folded neatly and deposited into the trash can. And the process is repeated for every dish, every meal, every day.

It exhausts me to watch. I couldn't imagine denying my little garbage disposal the treat of happily consuming the leftovers from our plates. If I didn't feed the thing, I would feel downright neglectful in my duties as a domestic goddess.

Another friend is very strict about food preparation. She believes no food should be touched by human hands. Nothing should touch cookie batter but plastic, metal, or glass—no fingers, not even a toothpick if it has been dunked in batter once before. So when she makes thumbprint cookies, she uses a spoon to create the indentation in the dough, when most of us rational beings would just use our thumbs.

Now, I've tried to talk sense into the woman. We've had many discussions in her kitchen and mine. "They are *thumbprint* cookies, for goodness' sake. You are supposed to use your thumb! It says so in the recipe." Not that I always follow recipes exactly, but she does, so that is a good argument. Undeterred, she continues to insist on using a spoon. She has even purchased itty-bitty spoons from Ikea for the job.

To be fair to our friendship, I decided to process it more before nagging her about the cookies again. I am not sure why it bothers me, but it does. Can it really matter what makes the indentation as long as the ooey, gooey jam is spooned into the middle (which legitimately does require a spoon)? Don't the cookies taste the same either way? They're made of sugar, flour, and butter. What is the importance of a thumbprint?

If I were a cookie, would it matter where the imprint came from? I know, that may not be a normal question. But really, whose imprint would I want on me? An imprint can come from many possible sources—parents, life experience, the world, ancestors, or neighborhoods. If I am imprinted, I think the details of its origin matter a great deal.

I want to be imprinted by God. I want to be so obviously marked by Him that you can see the ridges of His fingerprints on my life. I want no question about Who made me. If I were a cookie, it might not matter. But as a Christian, it does. "If we live, we live for the Lord; and if we die, we die for the Lord. So, whether we live or die, we belong to the Lord" (Romans 14:8, NIV).

Whether cookies are made with thumbs or spoons doesn't change the result or the taste. So . . . I let that go. But every time I eat a thumbprint cookie, I remember the lesson from our cookie conversation. We all have been made in different ways, but the result is the same: We belong to God. My job is to let the imprint of God show through in everything I do, even when baking cookies.

Dear God, please put Your imprint on my life. Mark me as unmistakably Yours. When people look at my life, let them see Your fingerprints all over it. Let there be no part—not one crumb—that isn't identifiable as Yours.

SPOON-PRINT COOKIES

If you have an aversion to touching your food, a small spoon works wonderfully for this recipe. If you don't, stick that thumb right on in there! Either way they are scrumdiddlyumptious. I fill mine with homemade jelly made with blackberries from my cousin's patch!

Ingredients

⅔ cup butter or margarine
1½ cups all-purpose flour
½ cup sugar
2 egg yolks
1 teaspoon vanilla
½ teaspoon salt
⅓ to ½ cup strawberry, apricot, or blackberry preserves or jelly

Instructions

1. Preheat oven to 375 degrees.
2. In a mixing bowl, beat butter or margarine with an electric mixer on medium to high speed for 30 seconds.
3. Add about half of the flour as well as the sugar, egg yolks, vanilla, and salt. Beat until thoroughly combined. Beat in remaining flour. Cover and chill for about 1 hour or until easy to handle.
4. Shape dough into 1-inch balls. Place 1 inch apart on a cookie sheet lined with parchment paper.
5. Press centers with your thumb or a round spoon (like a 1-teaspoon measuring spoon) to make an indentation to hold preserves later.
6. Bake for 10 minutes. Remove from oven and fill centers with preserves or jelly.
7. Return to oven and bake an additional 6–8 minutes, until the edges are lightly browned.
8. Cool cookies on a wire rack. Makes about 20 cookies.

Values are like fingerprints.
Nobody's are the same,
but you leave 'em all over
everything you do.

ATTRIBUTED TO ELVIS PRESLEY

LISTEN

Don't just listen to God's word.
You must do what it says.
JAMES 1:22

I heard giggles and whispers as I made my way to the kitchen. Three sweet girls were trying to make cookies. They had finally settled on a recipe but needed to locate the ingredients. Not knowing where things were, they asked me to point out what was what. All the baking supplies were in big jars without labels: flour, sugar, powdered sugar, brown sugar. Amid the giggles, I pointed out the correct jars and left the girls to their task since they were old enough to handle the oven.

A little while later, I heard, "Mom! Mom! Come here."

Their batter looked fine, but instead of individual cookies, a thin sheet of a cookie substance came out of the oven in crispy strips. When we bit into them, they were sweeter than Alabama sweet tea. It was a toothache in a pan! Something was off-kilter.

"Mom, why don't these taste like yours?"

I looked around and realized the powdered sugar was very low in its jar.

"Um, did you use this jar as flour?"

"Yes! You said to use the flour in the jar."

I had given that instruction while pointing to a different jar. They were too busy giggling and whispering to really hear what I was saying or to look where I was pointing.

"Well, you've created a new cookie recipe—sugar crisps. Maybe it will become a thing."

They had another fit of giggles before skedaddling with the cookie crunchies to watch television.

They hadn't listened closely enough. It wasn't a big deal. But what happens when it is? What happens if the instructions are important, or if directions are needed to keep from getting lost? What happens if it's God talking?

We read the Bible and listen to God's Word in church or on our apps. But are we really listening? Do we understand the promises? Are we heeding the warnings? Are we following the directions? Do we pay enough attention to carry our Sunday instructions into our Monday lives?

Or are we, like the girls making cookies, building a recipe for life that is lacking a key ingredient?

How do we train our brains to give thanks, be patient, or love unconditionally when the recycling bin is overflowing onto the floor? When bills outdistance paychecks? When the cat food can is sitting on the counter drawing flies while the kids dance right by it, listening to their favorite playlists? It isn't easy to remember Sunday's message then.

God didn't promise it would be easy. But He did say He would help and that it would be worth the effort. James gives us the key to getting through it: "Come close to God, and God will come close to you" (James 4:8).

We are not alone in this. We have help. We simply need to mosey on up and ask Him for it—and then listen to His answer. The more we read God's Word and talk to and listen to Him in prayer, the easier thanksgiving, patience, and love will come.

We can do that.

Listen—really listen. Follow directions. Do the things. Eat a cookie.

That's the recipe for a beautiful life.

Dear Father, thank You for bringing the sweetness of Your Word into my life. Help me to not only hear You but also focus on Your words and where You are pointing—every day of the week. Come close to me, Father, even when I am not listening. Open my ears and eyes to hear and see You better.

CHOCOLATE CHIP COOKIE CRISPS

Like the cookies the girls accidentally made, these are crisp, sweet cookies. Not slap-your-momma sweet; more like you-might-want-to-let-those-trousers-out-a-smidge sweet.

Ingredients

1⅓ cups all-purpose flour
½ teaspoon baking soda
¼ teaspoon salt
½ cup unsalted butter, melted and cooled
½ cup powdered sugar
⅓ cup packed light brown sugar
2 tablespoons light corn syrup
1 large egg
1 tablespoon milk
1 teaspoon vanilla extract
1 cup semisweet chocolate chunks

Instructions

1. Preheat oven to 350 degrees. Line large baking sheets with parchment paper.
2. In a medium bowl, whisk together the flour, baking soda, and salt.
3. In a large bowl, vigorously beat the butter, powdered sugar, brown sugar, and corn syrup with a spatula until very well combined. Add the egg, milk, and vanilla and beat vigorously until well mixed. Gradually add the flour mixture and stir until just combined, being careful not to overmix. Gently stir in the chocolate chunks. The dough will be very loose and sticky and more like batter in consistency.
4. Using a small scoop, drop dough onto the prepared baking sheets, spacing at least 2 inches apart. Bake for about 12 minutes or until golden brown and flat, rotating the sheets halfway through baking. Bake one sheet at a time for even cooking.
5. Let cookies cool on the baking sheets for 5 minutes; then use a thin spatula to move to wire racks to cool completely. Store in an airtight container for up to 5 days at room temperature. If desired, reheat the cookies in a 350-degree oven for 3–5 minutes, or until warmed through.

A SCONE BY ANY OTHER NAME . . .

*Now the LORD God had formed out of the ground all the wild
animals and all the birds in the sky. He brought them to the
man to see what he would name them; and whatever the man
called each living creature, that was its name.*

GENESIS 2:19, NIV

Children have a fondness for naming. They name their
dolls, trucks, blankies, and building blocks. "Where
is Wilma?" or "I want a Warry" (Larry the Cucumber, of
VeggieTales fame) are things I heard as a mom when my kids
were looking for toys or telling me what they wanted for lunch.

In our kitchen, lots of inanimate objects were named.
Plants, pots, chairs, food. The stew, the frittata, the scones—
they all had names. To this day, my now-adult children will ask
if I am making James Earl Scones or Hakuna Frittata for the
holidays (*Hakuna Frittata*—what a wonderful phrase!)—and
singing ensues.

It is not only children who have naming relationships with
inanimate objects. One of my friends names all her plants,
including her Christmas tree. She talks to them when she
walks through the house to get morning coffee and says good
night to them as she is checking doors and turning out lights.
Because what Christmas tree doesn't need a cheerful greeting
or wellness check? Another friend spends considerable time
deciding on a name for each car. Every one gets a new and

166

significant name according to the color, shape, and feel of the thing. Bless her heart.

Do you name things? It seems second nature to most of us (like Southerners painting their porch ceilings blue). It signifies ownership and intimacy. I mean, who wouldn't rather have a conversation with "Willamina" instead of with a doll that's like every other doll in every other house in every other town in America?

Naming identifies something as different, special, ours. It is intimately known by its Namer. It may not be perfect or grand or significant to anyone else, but the Namer knows it. Naming is personal and emotional.

In Isaiah 43:1, God says, "I have called you by name; you are mine." The chapter explains how well God knows us. It tells of the lengths He will go to protect us because He knows us so well. Our relationship with Him is personal and intimate. He declares that no one knows us or loves us as much as He does.

I never really thought about where the naming tendency comes from until recently. But it has always been there. God names. He built that naming instinct into Adam, and Adam has passed it along to us. We name, but more than that—we are named. We are His. We belong to the Name that is above all names. He loves us enough to name us and call us by name— even if we are missing an ingredient or two.

Lord, thank You for knowing me by name. Thank You for calling me Yours. My most precious name is Christ-follower. Help me to stay true to that name. Lord, I name You my King, now and forever.

I have called you by name;
you are mine.

ISAIAH 43:1

JAMES EARL SCONES

These delicious scones are best served fresh or the same day. They
have a crunchy outside and a tender, sweet interior no matter what
you call them. The recipe is based on one my sister-in-law Julie
shared with me many years ago.

Ingredients

Scones
1¾ cups self-rising flour
¼ cup sugar
¼ teaspoon salt
¼ cup cold butter, plus extra for cookie sheet
½ cup dried cranberries
½ cup white chocolate chips
½ cup Greek yogurt, plain or vanilla
⅓ cup buttermilk

Topping
1–2 tablespoons buttermilk
1 tablespoon raw (turbinado) sugar

Instructions

1. Preheat oven to 375 degrees. Stir together flour, sugar, and salt.
   With pastry blender, cut in ¼ cup cold butter until mixture
   resembles coarse crumbs.
2. Stir in cranberries and white chocolate chips. Mix yogurt and ⅓
   cup buttermilk in a small bowl until blended, then add to flour/
   cranberry/white chocolate chip mixture. Stir just until dry
   ingredients are moistened.
3. Rub a thin layer of butter on cookie sheet (or a pizza stone works
   great). Shape dough into a ball and place on cookie sheet. With
   floured fingers, press or roll dough into an 8-inch round. Cut
   into 8 pie-shaped wedges, but do not separate.
4. Brush dough with 1–2 tablespoons buttermilk. Sprinkle liberally
   with raw sugar.
5. Bake about 20 minutes or until edges are golden brown and center
   looks just set. Remove immediately from cookie sheet. Cool 5 minutes, then cut through the wedges to separate.

   Note: These are best eaten warm the day they are made. If eating
   later, reheat in an oven or toaster oven for a few minutes.

KEEP YOUR EYES PEELED

*Sin shall no longer be your master, because you are
not under the law, but under grace.*

ROMANS 6:14, NIV

Have you ever made sourdough starter? You mix a little
flour and water together in a big ole mason jar and wait.
Before long, wild yeast finagles its way into the mixture and
sets it to fussin' and bubblin' about. The mixture grows up
the sides of the jar, and then it shrinks. To help the yeast grow
strong, you have to keep feeding it a little flour and water.

It demands to be fed regularly, especially the first week.
Because of warmer temperatures, those of us in the South
usually need to feed our starter twice a day. It seems that every
time I turn around, it's time to feed the starter.

It is so needy, in fact, that if you choose to focus on something else, the starter will starve to death. I've thrown out several jars of "didn't start" over the years. No matter what else is
demanding your attention, you can't forget to watch the starter.
I am a slave to the sourdough.

Starter and children have a lot in common. They always
need to be watched!

As soon as Joel, our second born, was mobile, our relationship with Poison Control began. He was not only capable of
scaling cabinets to the very top shelf but also as quiet as a
mouse in a room full of cats. It was unbelievable. Add to that
his ability to sniff out paint, chemicals, and pharmaceuticals

from two hundred feet away, and you understand why we were afraid to sleep. He had to be watched every second.

One day I took Jasmine and Joel to the park, and we laughed and played until the kids were exhausted. I carried eighteen-month-old Joel the last few blocks on the way home. Upon entering the house, I deposited him on the floor and stooped to remove Jasmine's shoes and help her out of her jacket. When I straightened up, surprise! Joel had disappeared. He had been out of my sight for less than a minute!

A quick search found him standing on the kitchen counter downing a bottle of vitamins from the top shelf of the upper cabinets. The bottle claimed to have a childproof cap. Apparently Joel hadn't read that.

I was able to get him to spit out the vitamins. They came out in one big, half-chewed ball. I called Poison Control *again*.

Did you know that Poison Control doesn't keep a record of crazy mom calls?

My husband, Jeff, and I had to keep our eyes peeled with Joel. He could go from playing with Legos on the floor to sitting on top of the entertainment center sucking on VCR cleaning fluid in under two minutes. He was sneakier than a snake.

Almost every time, thankfully, Poison Control's prescribed solution was to feed him ice cream. So the whole family would load up and head to the ice cream stand. Jasmine *loves* ice cream. We started wonderin' if she was feeding Joel chemicals so she could score ice cream! You can't trust a four-year-old.

Joel needed constant attention. By the grace of God, we always caught him and fed him ice cream in time, so he never had to go to a doctor or a hospital. But it nearly killed us keeping up constant surveillance.

We all get distracted or forget to pay attention from time to time. It may result in a trip to the ice cream shop or something much more serious.

In Romans 6, Paul says we have a choice about what gets our attention. Sin fusses at us until we neglect other things. It is like bubbling sourdough starter that demands our focus and hinders us from seeking what matters to God.

Those "other things" are not necessarily bad on their own—caring for others, making a living, or removing your toddler's shoes. But if we feed them at the expense of starving our souls, what are the consequences? Let's just say they are worse than licking a runny ice cream cone.

When we feed our souls through prayer and the Word of God, the results are even better than fresh-baked sourdough with apple butter: "Now that you've found you don't have to listen to sin tell you what to do, and have discovered the delight of listening to God telling you, what a surprise! A whole, healed, put-together life right now, with more and more of life on the way!" (Romans 6:22, MSG).

Now that is the kind of surprise I can live with!

Joel has finally gotten into something that doesn't require a call to the Poison Control Center—he has mastered making sourdough bread. He occasionally eats it with a side of ice cream.

Jesus, thank You for feeding my soul. You are the Bread of Life, and as much as I love a good loaf, I love You more. Speak to my heart and help me be mindful of how important being present and paying attention are each and every day. Surprise me with a full, healed, put-together life!

SOURDOUGH STARTER

This is how you make homemade yeast. It takes only water and flour and patience. This recipe is based on information gleaned from BiggerBolderBaking.com, adjusted from experience. At that website and many others, there are lots of good recipes for using the starter.

Ingredients

Starter
½ cup whole wheat flour
⅓ cup water (tap water is fine)

Feeding the Starter
½ cup unbleached all-purpose flour
⅓ cup water

Instructions

Day 1: Make starter. Combine ½ cup whole wheat flour and ⅓ cup water in a large, sealable glass jar. Mix until smooth and thick. Cover loosely and let it rest in a warm spot for 24 hours.

Day 2: Wait. Rest the starter in a warm spot for another 24 hours.

Day 3: Feed starter. Remove and discard half the starter by weighing it (if you like doing that sort of thing) or eyeballing it. Feed it by adding ½ cup all-purpose flour and ⅓ cup water to the jar. Mix until smooth. The texture should resemble yogurt. Add water if too thick, or flour if too thin. Cover loosely and let it rest in warm spot for another 24 hours.

Days 4, 5, and 6: More feeding. Repeat the feeding process at least once a day. As the yeast begins to develop, starter will rise, and bubbles will form throughout the culture. When the starter falls, it's time to feed it again. If yeast is bubbling up and falling quickly, feed it more often or put it in a cooler location.

Day 7: Ready to bake. The starter should have doubled in size from day 1. There will be bubbles of all sizes, and the texture will be spongy and fluffy. It should smell boozy, like fermentation, but not nasty. Test your starter by dropping a teaspoon into a jar of water; if it floats to the top, it is ready. If not, keep feeding it and check every day until it does float. It could take another week, depending on the temperature. When your starter is ready, try using it in one of the many sourdough recipes avaiable online. For the remaining starter, restart the feeding process at Day 3, or refrigerate it until you are ready to start the feeding process again.

This is a record of the ancestors of Jesus the Messiah,
a descendant of David and Abraham.

MATTHEW 1:1

"Did you know our great-grandpa Dunn was born out of wedlock? His momma got pregnant while she was helping her pregnant sister."

"Wait. What?"

"Apparently that was a thing back then. A girl would go to help her sister who was expecting and end up pregnant by her brother-in-law or someone else in the family," my cousin said with a shrug. "I read that it happened a lot."

"Do they know it was her brother-in-law? And why did I not know this before?"

"I believe it is bona fide information. And the fact it hasn't been trumpeted about since means . . . well, it means our ancestors were up to some hanky-panky."

That information slowed the game we were playing around the kitchen table. Everyone started asking questions at once. According to this family legend, Great-Grandpa Hillis Dunn would have more correctly been named Hillis Meyers. Dunn was his mother's maiden name.

My cousins, sister, and their husbands were discussing how neither side of our family really knew parts of our ancestry. Grandpa Gallaher had his mother's maiden name and no acknowledged father. And Great-Grandpa Dunn had the name of his stepfather. We were wondering aloud about what our last names should have been and what kin we didn't know about.

"Well, if you think that's weird, I ain't even who I am," said Rick, the husband of one of my cousins.

I do believe sweet tea came shooting from someone's nose.

It turns out he was adopted, and his birth father had a questionable birth certificate. We concluded, after much discussion and laughter, that all our ancestry was just too crisscrossed to figure out and that perhaps our colorful ancestors added zest and interest to the family tree.

Then the game lured us back into knocking each other's playing pieces off the board and eating more snacks.

As interesting as my biological ancestry is, DNA doesn't define who I am. I am Betty's daughter, Carolyn's sister, Julia's and Anna's granddaughter. I come from a big hillbilly family that scratched out a living from the rocky Missouri soil.

My grandpa Dunn ate leftover cornbread in milk almost every morning. My aunts, uncles, cousins, and brothers are mushroom-hunting competitors. We all share a fondness for fried taters. We are family. DNA can't change that.

I am also a child of God. God doesn't care who fathered my great-grandpa or whether my great-great-grandma was a floozy. Accepting Jesus as my Lord and Savior overrides any background information. God accepts us into the family no matter how messed up our genealogy may be. We are adopted into the lineage of Jesus by simply accepting His invitation.

Matthew begins his Gospel by establishing that Jesus is from the lineage of David and Abraham. That is of utmost importance in proving that Jesus fulfilled Bible prophecy. There's no question who Jesus' people were. There are a few questionable, if-you-were-my-grandpa-I-would-hide-you-under-the-porch kind of people in that lineage. But each link is right there in Matthew for all the world to see.

Those connections mattered to the Jewish community Matthew was writing to. They knew the prophecies. They were waiting for the Messiah, and He had to have all the correct links. Matthew shows the world that Jesus truly was a descendant of David.

His ancestry overwrites ours. Through Jesus, God has adopted us into His family. Our DNA may throw us a few curves, but Jesus' blood wiped out that DNA and replaced it with His. His blood is the only blood that matters. If we could make a spiritual family tree, there would be one line from us to Jesus. All our trees would look the same.

After that board game, we encouraged each other to have DNA testing in hopes of seeing our ancestry a little more clearly—maybe finding new connections or unearthing undiscovered branches of the family. But we know who our people are. DNA won't change that.

And because I belong to Jesus, I also know who my spiritual Father is. Digging into His background in the Bible makes for fascinating reading. You can be sure He is who He says He is!

Dear Father, thank You for adopting me into Your family. Thank You for giving me such amazing people, both biological and spiritual. Lord, help me to accept all members of the family, no matter how they arrived, and to share with them the love You have so freely shared with me.

PEACH COBBLER IMPOSTER

This cobbler starts out with a runny batter on the bottom and a layer of peaches on the top. But when it comes out of the oven, the peaches have sunk, and the crust has surrounded them in a cloud of cobbler goodness. Both my grandmas, Julia and Anna, had recipes for this quick, easy, and inexpensive cobbler—that doesn't look like a cobbler. The original recipe called for oleo instead of butter, as did most of the recipes from my grandparents' generation.

Ingredients

Peaches
1 quart sliced unsweetened peaches (can or jar), undrained
¾ cup granulated sugar
1 teaspoon almond extract
¼ teaspoon salt

Batter
6 tablespoons butter
1 cup self-rising flour
1 cup granulated sugar
¾ cup milk
⅓ cup slivered almonds

Instructions
1. Add the sliced peaches (with juice), ¾ cup sugar, almond extract, and salt to a bowl and stir to combine.
2. Preheat oven to 350 degrees. Slice butter into pieces and add to a 9 x 13 baking dish. Place in the oven while it preheats, allowing the butter to melt. Once melted, remove dish from oven.
3. In a large bowl, mix together flour and 1 cup sugar. Stir in the milk, just until combined. Pour the mixture into the baking dish, over the melted butter, and smooth it into an even layer.
4. Spoon the peaches over the batter. Sprinkle slivered almonds on top.
5. Bake for about 38–40 minutes. Serve warm with ice cream or whipped cream.

HAZMAT

He said to me, "My grace is sufficient for you,
for my power is made perfect in weakness."
Therefore I will boast all the more gladly about my
weaknesses, so that Christ's power may rest on me.
2 CORINTHIANS 12:9, NIV

I have never been considered a graceful person. With my flat feet and waddle walk, I can't be mistaken for, say, a dancer or a former debutante. But I have generally been considered coordinated and even (when I was younger) athletic.

Now, however, I have become the woman who burns herself, falls, drops things, cuts herself when cooking, and causes general mayhem to her personhood. Those who know me well offer to carry heavy objects for me, wear steel-toed shoes when I am working around the house, and keep a safe distance when I'm doing anything that involves hot bubbling oil. (My son has suggested goggles and a hazmat suit for when I'm working in the kitchen.)

At this point, I can't blame them. I have cut the tip of my finger off with a mandoline, set toast on fire, and scarred my toe with hot mashed potatoes (wearing sandals in the kitchen is not the best idea in my world).

To add insult to injury, I've become a wimp. I'm losing my strength. I need help opening jars. I tire more easily. My bones hurt. I have a recurring pain in my neck (both literally and figuratively). And we don't even want to talk about what eating the wrong food does to me. I often plan outings around my lunchtime, nap time, and energy levels. It's sad.

When did I become such a wimp? I know it happened sometime after I had kids and before last week. I suspect that between the youthful period of working out five times a week and the present four-naps-a-week scenario, wimpiness just plain ole snuck up on me. Blast it.

Wimpiness seems to have invaded my spiritual life too. I have been infected with wishy-washy, status quo, and "I'll get to it later." I used to be so fearless. Theological discussions with friends or strangers were something I looked forward to. Now I avoid most of them because "I don't have brain power." Missions trips were among my highest goals. Lately I can't seem to squeeze one into my schedule. I've become wimpy, wimpy, wimpy! (Who knew my destiny was to be a cheap paper towel?)

Sometimes circumstances deflect God's calling. We argue that we are too tired or too weak or too clumsy. But is that selling ourselves short? God uses wimps to change the world. He uses weakness. His best heroes have scars. Joseph was a bullied younger brother and then enslaved in Egypt, but he went on to save nations. Moses had a speech impediment and a late start, but he led his people to freedom. David was just a weak boy when he took down Goliath. If they can do it, maybe we can, too, in our own tired, accident-prone ways.

Believe it or not, despite the mishaps and accidents, I am actually considered a good cook and baker, so I keep cooking anyway—as much as possible, for as many people as possible. Even when tired, covered in Band-Aids, or hopping around on one foot. When doing what God has put in my heart to do, the mishaps may slow me down, but they don't dampen my enthusiasm. Cooking is what feeds my soul. What feeds yours?

God has promised us His power, and with that on our side, we can conquer just about anything—even hot mashed potatoes that dive-bomb our toes!

Dear Jesus, please use my weakness and wimpiness for Your glory. Sometimes strength is needed, but thank You for the times when my weaknesses open doors that strength never could. I trust You to give me what I need in every situation.

MEATLOAF CUPCAKES WITH MASHED POTATO ICING

This is the recipe I was making when I scarred my toes. I was putting the hot mashed potatoes into a piping bag and dropped some on my foot. Please be careful when doing your piping!

Ingredients

Cupcakes
2 eggs, beaten
2 pounds lean (80% or 90%) ground beef
1 cup panko bread crumbs
1 small red onion, finely chopped
1 tablespoon fresh parsley, coarsely chopped (or 1 teaspoon dried)
1 clove garlic, finely chopped
⅔ cup ketchup
2 teaspoons Worcestershire sauce
Salt and pepper

Mashed Potato Icing
6 large Yukon gold potatoes, peeled and cubed
¼ cup butter
¼ to ½ cup milk
1 tablespoon dry ranch dressing mix
Salt and pepper

Instructions

1. Grease 18 regular-sized cupcake wells with cooking spray. Preheat oven to 350 degrees.
2. Mix cupcake ingredients in a large bowl until just combined. Disperse evenly among cupcake wells, pressing mixture flat on top.
3. Bake 35–40 minutes or until meat thermometer placed in center of cupcakes reads 160 degrees. While cupcakes are baking, put potatoes in a large pot of cold water; liberally salt the water. Bring to a boil, then reduce to a simmer until potatoes are fork-tender.
4. When cupcakes are ready, remove from oven. Cool for about 5 minutes before transferring to a wire rack.
5. Drain potatoes and return to pot. Add butter and ¼ cup milk. With a hand mixer, combine mixture, adding milk as needed. Season with ranch dressing mix, salt, and pepper.
6. Spoon potatoes into a 10-inch piping bag with a large star tip (or ½-inch opening). Working from the outer edge to the center, pipe potatoes onto cupcakes using an upward circular movement. Optional: Broil iced cupcakes 4 inches from broiler element until slightly browned.

I've always wanted to throw a party where everyone comes with their mother's meatloaf. Everybody could evoke their mother's memory through her meatloaf.

DIANE SAWYER

SABBATH MODE

The seventh day is a Sabbath day of rest dedicated
to the LORD your God. On that day no one
in your household may do any work.

EXODUS 20:10

My husband surprised me with a gas double oven a few years ago. The baker inside me danced a jig. I had visions of sheet pans full of cookies, roasting turkeys with all the fixins, and dozens of loaves of bread. It had five racks and two temperature zones and gleamed like a new penny.

Hot diggity dog!

Other women want shoes or spa treatments or new outfits. I want gadgets, appliances, and cookbooks. My kids complain that I have more gadgets than sense. The aebleskiver pan, pizzelle maker, and raclette would agree! A few of these gadgets take careful practice to use correctly. It is very important to read directions.

When the oven was installed, I immediately curled up with a cup of coffee and the manual. Amid the technical specs and directions for the steam self-cleaning option came information for using the Sabbath mode.

The oven has a Sabbath mode! When engaged, it disables tones and lights and has the ability to continuously run for the whole Sabbath.

During the Sabbath, or Shabbat, some Jewish people refrain from any kind of work. That means they cannot turn on the oven or the lights or touch any of the buttons. They take their day of rest seriously. To help the Jewish community stay true to their beliefs, many appliances offer this option.

The instructions for using the Sabbath mode require a whole page of explanation. It is very detailed. The instructions for the Sabbath in the Bible also take up a lot of space. The Old Testament repeats the requirement many times: The seventh day is holy (Genesis 2:3). Take a rest (Leviticus 16:31). Do no work (Exodus 20:10). And, "You shall kindle no fire throughout your dwellings on the Sabbath day" (Exodus 35:3, NKJV). That explains the Sabbath mode.

If the Bible admonishes our rest, why aren't we resting? The oven has a mode, a setting, a predetermined way of behaving. Once set into motion, the programming takes over. Maybe that is what we need: A setting for rest. A predetermined behavior that we can't turn off. A mode for following the Word of God.

We often believe that rest comes after the work. Modern societies measure time by morning work, then evening rest. But when time began, it was evening first, then morning (Genesis 1:5). Rest before work. Rest to prepare for work, to let our bodies and minds gain the strength they need to get through the day.

When did it change? When did rest become something we proudly proclaim we can do without? "I pulled an all-nighter!" "I'll sleep when I'm dead." Or one I've heard a lot: "Rest is for sissies." No, it is for all—the good, bad, and ugly.

Why are we so muleheaded when it comes to following the Sabbath rule? Maybe we feel that to achieve the American dream we must work hard to get ahead. Perhaps we were raised in a religious culture that puts an emphasis on works or earning God's love. Possibly it is the result of modern society that runs 24-7.

Whatever the cause, the remedy is simple—rest and pray. Once rest becomes a habit, we can turn it on and forget it. And if I need something baked on the Sabbath, my oven has me covered.

Lord, thank You for setting the example of rest for us. When I am putting too much into my life and not making time for rest, please remind me how important rest is. I know I need it, but I seem to forget. Help me embrace the Sabbath and keep it holy.

SLOW COOKER SALSA CHICKEN

This isn't exactly a Sabbath meal, but it is something you can make while resting. You can even combine all the sauce ingredients in one bowl the day before. Then on the Sabbath, simply dump the chicken into the slow cooker, pour the prepared sauce over the chicken, and turn it on low. It gives both you and your oven a rest!

Ingredients

3 pounds boneless, skinless chicken meat (we prefer dark meat)
1 10.5-ounce can of cream of chicken soup
1 can of salsa (use the empty soup can to measure)
1 package taco seasoning
Optional: Prepared rice or beans or tortilla chips
Shredded cheese for topping

Instructions

1. Place chicken in slow cooker.
2. Add remaining ingredients.
3. Cover and cook on low for 6–7 hours.
4. Remove chicken and shred with two forks.
5. Put chicken back in sauce and cook for another 30 minutes.
6. Serve over rice, beans, or tortilla chips. Top with cheese. The leftovers make excellent tortilla roll-ups.

FLATTER THAN A FLITTER

When they had prayed, the place in which they were gathered
together was shaken, and they were all filled with the Holy
Spirit and continued to speak the word of God with boldness.
ACTS 4:31, ESV

I love making bread. The smell of the yeast, the feel of the dough as I knead it, the smooth ballooning loaf—it makes me happier than a pig in a mud puddle. The absolute best part of bread, however, is watching the steam rise when you break apart a loaf right before you pop a bite into your mouth.

Because of my love of bread, yeast is a staple in my fridge. It comes out when I make cinnamon rolls, focaccia, pizza dough, or other yeasty, yummy goodness. That love for yeast breads and pastries has resulted in the perpetual backup yeast in the freezer.

Sometimes yeast doesn't rise: The water is too hot or too cold. Other ingredients—like salt—impede the activation process. Or the yeast itself has simply lost its spunk from waiting too long to be used.

That is what happened one night while I was preparing dinner for sixteen people. I put the yeast into water, and nothing. No bubbles. No happy yeasty smell. No gassy excitement. This was my backup yeast!

There wasn't time to start over, so I went ahead with the recipe. I mixed, kneaded, oiled, and put the bread in a proofing oven. When I took it out, it was flatter than a flitter. I wanted to breathe some air into it. But at that point there was very little I could do—the rest of the meal had been prepped.

I hoped and prayed the yeast would surprise me and rise up in the oven. I very carefully placed the dough in the oven, waited the allotted time, and pulled it out.

No surprises.

I brushed it with garlic butter and called it flatbread! It was a hit.

Without yeast, all bread is flatbread. Without the Holy Spirit, our spiritual lives are just as flat.

When I was growing up, the Holy Spirit was called the Holy Ghost. Back then most people read the King James Version of the Bible. Ghost meant something different when the KJV was translated, something like the "essence of one's being": "He breathed on them, and saith unto them, Receive ye the Holy Ghost" (John 20:22, KJV). When connotations changed, Bible scholars changed "Ghost" to "Spirit."

Back in the day, in the tiny church I went to, we had services where the Holy Ghost got ahold of someone, and we all witnessed it. One sweet lady would start walking the aisle of the church, swinging her arms and gettin' all happy about Jesus. And we were a conservative Baptist church. The Spirit has a way of moving people.

To take advantage of what the Holy Spirit offers, however, we must be prepared to receive Him. Hot tempers or cold hearts keep us from having Holy Spirit wisdom. Filling our lives with anxiety and stress hinders Holy Spirit growth. Putting off quality time with spiritual disciplines reduces Holy Spirit power.

When it comes to my spiritual walk, I want the power, growth, and wisdom that comes from being filled with the Holy Spirit. Daily. Hourly. Every moment if possible. I am trying to regulate my temperature, reduce things that interfere, and spend more time with God. My life is flatter than a flitter without it.

Heavenly Father, thank You for sending the Holy Spirit as my friend, comforter, and teacher. Open my heart and soul to grow through Your Holy Spirit guidance. Please keep my spiritual life activated by the power of the Holy Spirit within me.

ROSEMARY FOCACCIA

This is the bread I was making when my yeast failed me. It is flatter than most yeast breads, but not as flat as a flitter. It is great with salad or soup or toasted and dipped in Leftover Pinto Dip (see page 43).

Ingredients

2 cups warm water (about 110 degrees)
2 tablespoons active dry yeast (a little less than 3 packages)
2 tablespoons honey or sugar
2 cups bread flour (or use all-purpose flour)
2½–3 cups all-purpose flour, plus additional for kneading
1½ tablespoons kosher salt
2 tablespoons olive oil, plus extra for drizzling
2 tablespoons rosemary, roughly chopped
Flaked or crystal salt (about a teaspoon)

Instructions

1. Combine the water, yeast, and honey in a small bowl. Put in a warm place until yeast bubbles—about 5 minutes.
2. In the bowl of a mixer fitted with a dough hook, combine bread flour and 2 cups of all-purpose flour, kosher salt, olive oil, rosemary (save some for the top), and the yeast mixture on low speed. Add in more flour until the dough comes together.
3. Continue to knead with dough hook for 5–6 minutes on medium speed or on a floured surface for 8–10 minutes, until it becomes smooth and elastic. Add flour until dough is no longer sticky.
4. Transfer dough to a clean, lightly floured surface and shape into a ball. Sprinkle with flour and knead a few times if too sticky.
5. Lightly coat the inside of a lidded bowl with olive oil and put the dough in the bowl. Attach the lid and put in a warm place until doubled in size—about an hour. Punch down and divide into two pieces, shaping each into a rough circle.
6. Dust two baking pans with cornmeal. (I use round pizza pans.) Press each circle of dough out to fit the size of the pan.
7. Drizzle top with olive oil. Press your fingers into the dough, denting the entire surface. Cover loosely with a towel or plastic wrap. Let rise until it has doubled in size—about 45 minutes. Preheat the oven to 550 degrees (or as hot as your oven goes).
8. Lightly sprinkle the top with a drizzle of olive oil, extra rosemary, and a little flaked salt or salt crystals. Bake until the top of the loaf is golden brown—about 10 minutes. Remove from the oven and let cool before cutting and serving.

TOAST FLAMBÉ

Smoke, nothing but smoke. [That's what the Quester says.]
There's nothing to anything—it's all smoke.
ECCLESIASTES 1:2, MSG

"Um, your oven is on fire," my friend calmly pointed out. Sure enough, a fire was leaping and dancing inside the oven. I opened the door and just stared at it for a moment. The bread inside flamed like logs on a fire. We could have roasted marshmallows.

Reality kicked in when flames licked out and threatened my hair. I grabbed some mitts, pulled the burning pan from the oven, and ran it out to the grill. Slamming the lid shut, I turned to find my helpful friends videoing the whole thing.

Fast thinking on their part.

This wasn't the first time something had caught fire in my oven. There was the chicken thighs incident my church group reminds me about regularly (as if social media would ever let me forget). And the scone episode.

The bread was supposed to be the base for avocado toast we were making during a girlfriends' baking day. That idea went up in smoke. In my defense, one of the girls was telling a story about how she accidentally threw a party when she was in college and had to glue carpet fibers one-by-one into the burned area of her parents' living room carpet after the party

192

got out of hand. I mean, who remembers to check on plain ole toast when stories are that good?

We opened the windows, turned on a fan, and assessed the damage. It was minimal, so I cleaned out the oven, and we baked on.

When I was in junior high school, I awoke one night to flames and smoke raging outside my window. It scared the daylights out of me! My thoughts ran wild: *This is the end of the world! The Rapture has come! Or wait—maybe a band of Satan's followers are here to take over the world!*

When I screwed up the courage to look out the window, I saw my aunt's trailer, which had recently been wheeled into the field next to our yard, burning like a giant's bonfire. I started hollering so loud I nearly brought down the roof. I think I scared a few years off my family's lives. We formed a water brigade, bringing water up from the creek, but it was too late. Within minutes, there was nothing more than a sooty, smoking heap where her trailer had stood only an hour before. Thankfully, no one was home. But after that, there was no home to go to.

It can feel like the end of the world when our lives catch on fire or our dreams go up in smoke. Our first instinct is to imagine the worst. Like the writer of Ecclesiastes, we lament and question, *What's the use of it all?* It is hard to pick up the pieces and move forward.

But smoke can also be an indication of blessing. After all, God provided what fueled the fire: "When God gives someone wealth and possessions, and the ability to enjoy them, to accept their lot and be happy in their toil—this is a gift of God" (Ecclesiastes 5:19, NIV).

All those things that went up in smoke were gifts. They weren't useless, and we aren't alone. We have a Father who provides. He will protect, guide, and love us, even if we lose toast, jobs, or homes. Being healthy enough to enjoy life, to have a faith built from reliance on Him, to find joy even when we feel burned—these are gifts we can hold on to.

Life is more than smoke. It is friends, joy, laughter, blessings, and, on really good days, avocado toast.

Thank You, Lord, for keeping me and my friends and family safe from the figurative and literal fires in our lives. If I ever start complaining that life is nothing but smoke, remind me of the blessing of Your presence, provision, and restoration.

AVOCADO TOAST

Avocado toast is a recent culinary trend. As a child, I didn't know what avocados were. We sure didn't have them in the grocery stores in Reynolds County. Now they are readily available almost everywhere. Healthy. Versatile. Yummy.

Ingredients

2 slices of bread
1 avocado, peeled and mashed
½ lime, juice only
Garlic salt
Red pepper flakes

Optional
2 eggs, sunny-side up

Instructions

1. Toast 2 slices of bread in a toaster until golden and crispy. (If you double or triple this recipe, like we did, you can toast the bread under your broiler for a minute or two. Just be very, very mindful so it doesn't burn!)
2. In a small bowl, combine the avocado, lime, and garlic salt.
3. Spread half the mixture on each slice of toasted bread.
4. Sprinkle red pepper flakes over avocado. Top with egg if desired.

* Note: Pair this toast with Hominy Soup (page 53), and you'll be living in high cotton!

NO MORE DOT-COM MOM

Because this widow keeps bothering me,
I will give her justice, so that she will not
beat me down by her continual coming.
LUKE 18:5, ESV

When our children were young, most nights saw me working at my computer long after the kids were asleep. There were stories to write and deadlines to meet. I would put the kids to bed and then, with snack and a big glass of iced tea in hand, head to my home office in the basement.

Our youngest, Jackie, who was about three, slept with my husband and me at that time. We had just made a big move, and he didn't feel secure enough to stay in his new big-boy bed.

One night I heard the little *bump, scoot, bump, scoot* that meant he was scooching his way down the steps to see me.

"What's up, Little Guy? You should be asleep."

He peered around the door, slipped his thumb from his mouth, and said, "Come bed, Momma."

"I'll be there in a few minutes. Go back to bed."

With his little blankie trailing behind him, he slowly climbed back up the stairs—only to repeat the exercise five minutes later. On his third trip down, he pushed aside the door and crawled up in my lap. He put a fat little baby hand on each side of my face, looked into my eyes, and said, "No more dot-com, Mom. Pwease?"

That was that. Off to bed we went.

Pesky persistence pays off. In Luke 18:1-8, Jesus tells a story about a widow who kept going to a corrupt judge to ask for justice. The judge got tired of the woman asking over and over again, so he granted her request—even though he felt no moral obligation to do so. He wasn't a God-follower. He didn't care about the woman. He just wanted her to stop showing up in his courtroom.

"God will surely give justice to his chosen people who cry out to him day and night," Jesus explains in verse 7. He wants us to ask and ask again. To cry out night and day. To never give up requesting things like justice and protection and guidance and mercy.

Asking shows faith. It says we live in expectation of a just answer.

My son kept asking because he knew I would snuggle with him until he fell asleep. He trusted that I loved him enough to help him with what he couldn't accomplish himself. He didn't feel unloved when I didn't go up the first two times. My timing was different from his. But in the end, his expectation, his belief in my love for him, and his perseverance proved stronger than the pull of my work, and I followed him up those stairs.

Once I knew how important it was to him, how much he truly needed me with him, I responded. God does the same with us. He wants to know what matters to us, what we need, how He can soothe and comfort us. Our persistence shows faith and expectation. He is our hope.

Keep asking. God will answer.

Heavenly Father, thank You for listening to my cries. Thank You for answering my questions and demonstrating justice. Help me to always have faith in You and never stop asking for help with the things I can't accomplish myself.

DOT-COM POPCORN

This popcorn is deceptively simple. But it will give you the munch power you need to get through a long night at the computer—or a long movie with the kids! It is also a very good option for packaging up as a Christmas gift or including in an Easter basket.

Ingredients

$\frac{1}{4}$ cup coconut oil, or whatever oil you have

$\frac{1}{2}$ cup popcorn kernels

$\frac{1}{4}$ cup sugar

$\frac{1}{2}$ teaspoon salt

$\frac{3}{4}$ cup white chocolate chips or melting wafers

$\frac{1}{4}$ cup sprinkles

Instructions

1. Heat the oil in a 3-quart thick-bottomed saucepan on medium-high heat.
2. Put 3 or 4 popcorn kernels into the oil. Wait for them to pop before adding the rest of the kernels in an even layer. Sprinkle sugar over kernels.
3. Cover the pot and remove from heat for 30 seconds.
4. Return the pan to the heat, gently shaking the pan back and forth over the burner.
5. Keep the lid slightly ajar to let the steam from the popcorn release.
6. Once the popping slows to several seconds between pops, remove the pan from the heat, take off the lid, and dump the popcorn immediately into a wide bowl. (Because the sugar caramelizes, the popcorn is very hot. Resist the urge to try a piece right away. I learned that lesson for you.)
7. Sprinkle salt over the popcorn.
8. Melt white chocolate in a microwave-safe bowl for 30 seconds. Let sit for 10 seconds. Stir. Continue microwaving in 10-second increments, then stirring, until chocolate is melted.
9. Pour chocolate over popcorn. Add sprinkles.
10. Mix immediately with a large spoon until popcorn is coated. Spread popcorn out on a large cookie sheet and place in the fridge or freezer for a moment to let the chocolate harden. Store in an airtight container. Try not to eat it all in one sitting!

If you keep knocking long enough,
(your friend) will get up and give
you whatever you need because
of your shameless persistence.

LUKE 11:8

THANK YOU KINDLY

It is impossible to convey my absolute gratitude for those who supported, prodded, prayed for, encouraged, and pushed me to finally write this book. You know who you are. Thank you, from the bottom of my heart!

But in an attempt to recognize those who were essential . . .

This book would not exist without my agent, Cynthia Ruchti. Wow. Thank you for the push and the patience. You truly are a miracle worker.

Jeff, no one has ever believed in, supported, or cheered for me as much as you. I am overwhelmed with gratitude.

Lynn, you are the BFF everyone needs in their life. Your loving loyalty has ever been the wind beneath my wings.

Jasmine, Joel, and Jackie, thank you for making me laugh and forcing me to be the grown-up. But now it is your turn.

Heather and Randi, thank you for never doubting the process and for listening to my stories—when I could get a word in!

Cat, thank you for professional advice and guidance from the heart. You truly made a difference in this book!

Darla and the Six Sisters, your prayers guided everything.

Becky Brandvik, my Tyndale publisher, thank you for taking a chance on my little hillbilly manuscript. Your enthusiasm made me believe in it all the more.

Anisa Baker, thank you for making the editing process a dream! Your kind words and thoughtful suggestions were transformative.

Mom, Everett, Carolyn, Mike, and Virgil, thank you for letting me live to tell these stories. I know I sorely tested your patience. Loving you and being your family has been my great honor.

Finally, thank you to my large, loud hillbilly family—what a legacy you have given me! Grandma Dunn set the bar high with her table overladen with food and her heart overflowing with love. But from the oldest uncles to the youngest cousins, you have allowed her legacy to live on. Thank you. Thank you kindly.

ABOUT THE AUTHOR

Marilyn Jansen has been writing and creating since she glued dandelions into her first book at age four. She has been an editor in Christian publishing since 1998 and has contributed—either as developer, writer, or editor—to hundreds of Christian books and journals, both in-house and freelance. She is editorial director of the gift department of Harper Collins Christian Publishing. As co-owner of Nashville Cooks, Marilyn writes about Music City's diverse food scene and contributes recipes inspired by those menus. She has three adult children and lives in Nashville, Tennessee.